Praise for *Place Your Thoughts Here*

"*Place Your Thoughts Here* is truly unique in the way it guides the reader to a landing zone: a place to begin our creative journey. It inspires us to discover the source of unselfconscious spontaneity and the nature of beauty. Any artist, or anyone with aspirations of being one, must read this book!"
  —Stanley Weiser, screenwriter for *Wall Street*,
    W, and *Freedom Song*

"Through the lens of Buddhism, Steven Saitzyk taps into the human need to create. This is a handbook for clearing one's mind so the creative process can blossom. *Place Your Thoughts Here* is a valuable resource for artists and CEOs alike because, after all, creativity is at the core of all human endeavors."
  —John Millei, visual artist

"When I'm standing before a live audience and about to improvise a solo, how do I avoid becoming a deer in the headlights? By simply being myself, in the moment, smiling at the possibilities and taking the leap! That's what *Place Your Thoughts Here* reaffirms. Steven Saitzyk uses examples of the common perceptions about artists, art making, and experiencing art to assist in a deeper understanding of where our meditation practice might take us or what it might open our hearts and minds to."
  —Michael Doucet, musician, composer,
    United States Artists Award recipient

Place Your Thoughts Here

Meditation for the Creative Mind

Place Your Thoughts Here

Meditation for the Creative Mind

Steven Saitzyk

First Thought Press
Los Angeles

First Thought Press

Los Angeles, CA

© 2013 Steven Saitzyk

Author photo © Jason Elias

"Place your thoughts here," cover art by Steven Saitzyk, watercolor, 2009.

"A Dot in Space" (translated from Tibetan) by Vidyadhara Chögyam Trungpa Rinpoche, 24 ¼ x 35 in. Calligraphy executed in author's studio in Venice, California. 1980. Author's collection.

"Kongo" or "Vajra" in Sanskrit, "Diamond-like" in English, by Taizen Maezumi Roshi, 25 ½ x 51 in. 1980. Author's collection.

"The Buddhist Goddess Sita Tara" (White Tara), 19th century. Central Tibet, Gelupa Monastery, Himalayas. Painting; Thangka, Mineral Pigments and gold on cotton cloth; silk borders, 32 ¾ x 21 in. Gift of Mrs. Anna C. Walter (M.82.233) Los Angeles County Museum of Art, Los Angeles, CA. Digital Image © 2009 Museum Associates / LACMA / Art Resource, NY.

"Shri" (Palden Llamo), circa 1750-1850. Central Tibet, Himalayas. Painting: Thangka, Mineral Pigments and gold on Cotton cloth, 28 ½ x 21 ¼ in. From the Nasli and Alice Heeramaneck Collection, Museum Associates Purchase (M.83.105.17) Los Angeles County Museum of Art, Los Angeles, CA. Digital Image © 2009 Museum Associates / LACMA / Art Resource, NY.

"Woman Holding a Balance" by Johannes Vermeer, Widener Collection, Image courtesy of the Board of Trustees, National Gallery of Art, Washington, c. 1664, oil on canvas, stretcher size: 16 ¾ x 15; painted surface 15 7/8 x 14.

"Primordial Buddha Samantabhadra in mystical embrace with his consort Samantabhadri." Tibetan banner. Coll. Maraini, Florence, Italy. Photo Credit: Scala / Art Resource, NY.

"The Five Elements," Calligraphy by Sakyong Mipham Rinpoche, 22 x 30 in., 2004. Author's collection.

Mandala of Kalachakra (wheel of time). Tibetan tangka, 18th century. Tempera on fabric, 94 x 71 cm. Musee des Arts Asiatiques-Guimet, Paris, France. Photo Credit: Réunion des Musées Nationaux / Art Resource, NY.

ISBN 978-0-9891454-0-4

10 9 8 7 6 5 4 3 2 1

This book is dedicated to: my root guru Chögyam Trungpa Rinpoche; my teacher Sakyong Mipham Rinpoche; my wife Anne, without whom this book would not have happened; and my son Brian, who inspires me.

Contents

Preface: Why I Wrote This Book   xi

Note to the Reader: Visual Examples and Calling Yourself
    an "Artist"   xiii

Foreword: The Profundity and Power of the Creative Mind   xv

Chapter One: A Place to Land   1

Chapter Two: The Importance of Doing Nothing   9

Chapter Three: Meditation Instruction   15

Chapter Four: Perception Is More Important Than Talent   27

Chapter Five: Felt Sense and Thought Sense   39

Chapter Six: Self-Expression and Pure Expression   47

Chapter Seven: Originality, Creativity, and Spontaneity   55

Chapter Eight: Signs and Symbols   65

Chapter Nine: The Creative Process as Meditation-in-Action   87

Chapter Ten: The Viewing Process   105

Chapter Eleven: Conditional and Unconditional Beauty   119

Chapter Twelve: Presence and the Sublime   135

Chapter Thirteen: The Power of Display   157

Notes   177

Acknowledgments   187

About the Author   189

Figures

Figure 1: "A Dot in Space" by Vidyadhara Chögyam Trungpa
Rinpoche, referring to the birth of inspiration   14

Figure 2: Square Table   28

Figure 3: Square Table in Perspective   29

Figure 4: Ambiguous Trident   32

Figure 5: "Kongo" or "Vajra" in Sanskrit, "Diamond-like"
in English, by Taizen Maezumi Roshi   64

Figure 6: Illustration of a Rose   70

Figure 7: No Smoking Symbol   78

Figure 8: White Tara, a Buddhist deity of peaceful compassion 130

Figure 9: Palden Lhamo, a Buddhist deity of wrathful compassion 131

Figure 10: Ever increasing and spinning Yin-Yang symbol   146

Figure 11: *Woman Holding a Balance* by Johannes Vermeer   148

Figure 12: Barely visible mirror on the wall under the window   149

Figure 13: Detail of the woman holding a balance   150

Figure 14: Detail showing the woman's face   151

Figure 15: Detail showing the Last Judgment   152

Figure 16: Samantabhadra and Samantabhadri in sexual union 154

Figure 17: *The Five Elements* by Sakyong Mipham Rinpoche   156

Figure 18: The Chinese character for "emperor"   164

Figure 19: Tibetan Buddhist Kalachakra sand mandala   165

Preface

Why I Wrote This Book

I t is said that most authors end up writing the book they would like to read. That is true here. For several decades I waited for someone to write this book so I could read it. While books have been written on the subject of meditation, art-viewing, or art-making, none combine them.

In 1974, I first glimpsed that it was possible to integrate art viewing and making with meditation. I met and began to study with Chögyam Trungpa Rinpoche, who was a Tibetan meditation master, teacher, and artist. He had studied art at Cambridge University, and when he came to the United States, Trungpa Rinpoche taught Buddhism to many students and established Naropa University and Shambhala. He truly was one of the great Buddhist teachers of our time.

The main gift Chögyam Trungpa Rinpoche offered was that he engaged the creative process from the inside out, whereas I was trying to work from the outside in. I was attempting to get to the experience of art, art-making, and the workings of the creative mind through information and ideas. Through him, I realized that my approach was more conceptual than real. In essence, Trungpa Rinpoche's approach was to see things as they are rather than merely thinking or imagining how they are. He taught us to directly experience art, art-making, and the nature of our minds.

Several decades later, after the passing of Trungpa Rinpoche and after developing my eclectic background of science, art, meditation, Buddhist philosophy and psychology, and teaching, I gave up my search for a book that doesn't exist and finally wrote this one. In doing so, I have felt the precious weight of what I have learned from my teachers and various artists I have worked with over the years, especially Chögyam Trungpa Rinpoche, Sakyong Mipham Rinpoche, Taizen Maezumi Roshi, Ed Moses, and Sam Francis. If I have learned anything and can manage to pass it on, I should follow their example and do so.

Even the most skilled teachers know that you don't really learn a subject until you have to teach it. Knowing a subject is easier than explaining it so others understand it. I have taught this material for a long time, led many field trips and salons, but articulating this subject in writing has been the most engaging and deepening means of learning.

Note to the Reader

Visual Examples and Calling Yourself an "Artist"

While I have engaged many creative disciplines, my experience is rooted in the visual arts. Therefore, many of the examples in this book reflect that. I have written this book so that regardless of your creative discipline, connecting with the visual examples is effortless. During my thirty-five years of teaching, I have seen cardiac surgeons, criminal defense attorneys, therapists, educators, and performers of all kinds benefit from the visual examples offered here. They engage music, dance, poetry, multi-media, or no formal discipline, and have shown me that bringing the insights that result to any form of creative engagement is natural and easy.

I sometimes run across students who claim that they are simply creative, but do not consider themselves artists. I use the labels "artist" and "art-maker" in this book, and I feel it is necessary to say that creativity and the creative mind is not the exclusive province of those who choose to make art. The creative process takes place all the time in everyday life situations. For example, we all need to figure out what to wear in the morning, contribute to interesting dinner conversations, purchase something decorative for our homes—and then find the right place for the object. Creativity also happens when we come up with a new strategy for our lives, a solution to a vexing problem, or when we are simply at play. Creativity and the creative mind are integral to our lives. Therefore—regardless of how we see ourselves—all of us are, in fact, artists.

Foreword by Sakyong Mipham Rinpoche

The Profundity and Power
of the Creative Mind

Author's note: *The Sakyong, Jamgön Mipham Rinpoche, is a Buddhist teacher who grew up in both the East and the West. The eldest son of Chögyam Trungpa Rinpoche, who was instrumental in bringing Buddhism to the West, he holds their family lineage as the head of the Shambhala, a global network of meditation and retreat centers that includes Naropa University. He is a poet and an artist who has authored many books, including* Turning the Mind into an Ally, Ruling Your World, Running with the Mind of Meditation, *and* The Shambala Principle. *He is my teacher as was his father, for which I am immeasurably grateful. The "dharma art" teachings described in the foreword below are the basis for many of the views and techniques described in this book.*

Dharma art teaches us how to re-empower our lives and the world. It challenges us as human beings to realize how numb we are and to reignite our appreciation of our surroundings. In the old days, people revered the elements because they were more susceptible to them. Their relationship with the world had profundity and power. In our own era, the kind of dignity from which dharma art arises is being disempowered because we have less and less direct contact with the elements. The teachings of dharma art have profundity and power because they wake us up to the magic of our own perceptions.

The Sanskrit word *dharma* literally means "truth." What is the truth? Phenomena and appearances are always changing against a backdrop of a more primordial awareness—self-existing, pristine natural energy. In practicing dharma art, we work with the phenomenal world in ways that help us discover and express that truth, which is perpetually slipping by. Penetrating it requires perception that is free of concept and judgment. Dharma art shows us how to perceive the world directly. In developing such perception, we are learning to identify with the profound simplicity of our own nature, which the Shambhala teachings call "basic goodness." This process is threatening to the ego, the sense of who we think we are. It begins with seeing the truth of impermanence.

When we know that what we see, hear, taste, touch, smell, and feel is transitory, we begin to understand impermanence. Ingraining this knowledge counteracts the notion of eternalism that shows up in our daily lives as trying to prolong our experience—our pleasure and even our pain. We want our experience to last. Through the process of extending it, we use our experience to solidify our sense of self—our view of the world and how we exist in it. Our desire to elongate and interpret our experience keeps us from engaging in what is happening presently.

In dharma art we break down this tendency to solidify the sense of who we think we are by relating with the moment. When we relax and let ourselves be in the ever-changing present, we don't have the opportunity to make things solid. Rather, we can actually see the elements in full display, like a flower in bloom. When the openness of our perception allows us to engage with the power of the moment, we can express impermanence spontaneously. So dharma art begins with training ourselves to relax with things as they are.

We initiate this process in meditation practice, during which we learn to watch our thoughts arise and fall without reacting, bringing our minds back to the breath. Such discipline trains us in connecting with the energy of basic goodness that is always underneath the impulse to solidify our perceptions and feelings. We begin to see that our perceptions are inhibited by a particular view of our own—"me"—that colors everything we do. We also begin to see that underneath all of our concepts and feelings, there is space that is available in any moment. This is the nature of ourselves as we are and things as they are.

"Things as they are" is dharma. Practicing meditation helps us develop the skillful means to perceive and express that truth directly with fresh minds. We can be happy and relaxed with what we have. Without seeing things as they are, it is hard to create art. Our perceptions are obscured and our minds are not fresh, so making art becomes a troubled, futile process by which we're trying to create something based on concept.

When we practice dharma art, there's a quality of freedom in the artistic process. Our art becomes something we discover rather than create. When we see ourselves and the world as transitory, we begin to relax, to look at what is happening with curiosity about where it leads. We don't have to try so hard. We let go. Now the real artisan begins to come out. We begin to have a pure perception, a perception based on no system, not even the system of "me." When we discover the natural level of perception that exists primordially and takes care of itself, when we are one with the objects that we perceive, then we have discovered dharma art. With a completely open mind, we appreciate all of our experiences equally. Now we can express the truth to others.

The practice of dharma art is a way to use our lives to communicate without confusion the primordial and magical nature of what we see, hear, and touch. It gives us the ability to communicate the awakened nature of our heart and mind through order and through chaos. Its principles can even be applied to how we dress and what we eat. As practitioners of this kind of art, we are committing ourselves to pointing out to people the nature of their own mind: basic goodness. That is what is appealing and powerful about these teachings. We can communicate basic goodness through symbol, which gives others the power to realize it instantaneously.

Earth, water, fire, air, and space—there's a tremendous range of communicative power within these elements. Communication is a two-way street that runs on harmony. Everybody has a different face and a different shape, but somehow our hearts are all very similar. Expressing with our heart, while understanding that we all have the same heart, creates the harmony to help people realize their elemental wisdom and compassion. The end result is greater freedom.

This is not to say that dharma art is an easy path. We must have a good balance between discipline and freedom—not too tight, not too loose—just as we do in meditation. Some of us pick up on the discipline and think that's it, and some try to pick up on the fluidity and easiness—the "I-couldn't-care-less" quality of it—and think that's it. But dharma art is about bringing proportion and balance between the two.

The practice of perceiving directly is the practice of meditation—total mindfulness of body, feeling, mind, and phenomena. As we tame the mind, we begin to realize that it is inseparable from our perception. We start looking at our experience precisely, without attachment. We see that it's right just the way it is. We resonate with it. Such moments of true perception, true communication, are liberating. Relaxing into the present moment has taken us beyond duality, beyond the notion of self.

Because we change and conditions change, dharma art is process and movement, not a fixed result. In flower arranging for example, we're not simply moving branches around—how we move them is important. The power lies in our engagement with what we are doing, even before the level of thought. Once we go through the process of developing pure perception, we can perceive the truth. This truth exists primordially. It exists momentarily. It exists all the time. Dharma art expresses the open, radiant energy that is pulsating within us and within everything around us all the time.

As artists, we think, "What about something new and radical?" Well, the whole thing has actually already happened. We can take it to fruition when we let go of confusion and appreciate our senses fully. Then we are free to empower objects with our understanding and use what we make to draw other people into a deep, elemental reality.

Chapter One

A Place to Land

Things are not difficult to make;
what is difficult is putting ourselves
in the state of mind to make them.

~ Constantin Brancusi[1]

"My creative process is a meditation." I have heard this statement often. While art-making and art-viewing are inherently contemplative activities, they are not the same as a meditation practice. They can parallel one another when they invoke a similar state of mind, but it is what makes them different that provides the ability for formal meditation practice to benefit the way we create and view art.

Meditation helps synchronize mind with body, right hemisphere of the brain with left, enhance intuitive and intellectual abilities, and promote clear perception. Much of art is about seeing and experiencing things as they truly are, and enjoying genuine spontaneity and unselfconscious, pure expression. Meditation helps us to better achieve this. It also dissolves creative blockages, reveals the source of creativity, and offers a path toward experiencing the sublime state in which our experience and knowledge merge into one.

Landing in the Right State of Mind

In the absence of a meditative discipline, we tend to create little rituals that we hope will lead to a starting point for our next project or recreate a state of mind to resume an existing one. We are looking for a specific state of mind, or place to land—and not just any place. Our ritual might involve making coffee, having a smoke, returning a phone call, checking email, reading the newspaper, or going for a walk or run. Some of us clean up the work space, organize our tools, spread out our materials, trash something, or scrutinize where we left off. For others among us, stress, excitement, sex, or drugs seem to take us to the states of mind we think we should be in before we can create. Whether we are on autopilot mentally, or focused like starving vultures, we're looking for an inner landing zone permeated with clarity and confidence. Until we are in that elusive place, we insist that we cannot begin to work meaningfully.

Whatever our personal flight plan is to get there, some of the activities we choose can end up becoming distractions, causing us to go off course or even crash land. We might get wired from drinking too much coffee, get caught up in an argumentative email, trash a project with real potential, or even become habituated or addicted. Distractions and sidetracks are limitless and our landing zones are frustratingly few. The truth is that trying too hard causes the zone to unpredictably slip out of reach or completely disappear. Nevertheless, we keep trying. The alternative is, well, there is no alternative. If there is no landing place, there is no creative process.

At this point, some among us push the envelope and fly even higher. I've seen many artists use exhaustion or panic as their home base for creating. With exhaustion, we dive into the distractions until they are depleted and we can only surrender. Panic involves not doing any work until it's near impossible to meet our deadline. At that point, evasions self-destruct because we are confronted with the terror of complete failure. But these methods usually come at a high physical and emotional cost, as documented—and in some cases romanticized—in lives of artists like Caravaggio, Pollock, Rothko, and countless others.

It can be so tiring and disappointing when what we want is so simple: to come home to that place, the zone, our starting point. All we want is a place where we are alive, awake, aware, energized, and not particularly self-conscious. We are happy when we get even a taste of that and ecstatic when we're fully there. But here's the strange thing: when we are fully there, we most often don't know it until we fall out of it and become self-conscious again. Our self-aware selves look back and realize we *were* there. We were there without self-dialoguing about it. We were immersed in the moment rather than separated from it by observing ourselves. It seems so natural when we are there and yet it can be such a challenge to get there. Why is that?

"Just be here now." This is advice many of us have heard. Intuitively, we know our landing place has everything to do with being in the moment. When we are in the now, there is no past or future. Even when our creative process involves drawing on our past history or our future possibilities, they are all brought into the present moment. We have not lost our minds to recollections or anticipations. It is an amazing concept when we think about just being here, but being here now is not a thought. It is an experience. So thinking, "be here now" will not get us to nowness and our landing zone where we can begin our creative process. We could think ourselves into moving toward such a moment, or we might recall being in such a moment, but we cannot create the experience of now with only a thought. It is as if there is not enough space for the experience and the thoughts about it to exist simultaneously. Familial and cultural conditioning, genetics, brain chemistry, lack of discipline or realization, as well as hope and fear all prevent us from being consistently in the now.

Try to be here now as you read this. Time yourself. How long before your mind drifts? Hours, minutes, seconds—or even less—pass. Where have you drifted to? Your grocery list, your next project, your relationships?

Is it hopeless? Are we shut out? Is it fate? Or is there a way we can increase the odds of finding our personal landing zone? Let's look at the reasons behind our personal precreative process, or rituals. Are they not about clearing the "cobwebs" away and waking ourselves up from our habitual daze? Most certainly, yes. They are also about detaching ourselves from what binds us to the past and future to create mental or physical space so there is room for something new to arise, to be seen and appreciated.

If our heads are filled with mental activity, there is no room for anything new to spontaneously arise. And, if something new manages to squeeze its way to the surface, it is likely to be crushed by the next thought stream. In their own way, our rituals are attempts to provide sufficient space for our incessant thought streams to slow down and become quiet. The key problem is that our rituals often end up feeding our thought streams rather than starving them. They become distractions themselves.

If our rituals are less effective than we would like, then we need new ones that truly lead us to the place we wish to be. Rituals like meditation, meditation-in-action, and the contemplations discussed in the following chapters, all offer the means for achieving sufficient space for distractions to dissolve while allowing originality to spontaneously arise. In other words, they help us find and come to rest in our landing zone.

Bringing a new or different ritual into our creative process can be a fearful prospect. Not because we fear it will not work, but because we fear letting go of the ritual we have in favor of a new one that we have not personally tested. Today, there are numerous articles and studies about how meditation benefits our minds and bodies, so you may be less concerned about whether meditation is effective than you are about whether you will be able to meditate.

An Artist's Fear of Meditation

Artists approach meditation with all kinds of preconceptions, doubts, and even fears. If you already have a meditation practice, you know there is nothing to fear from it. People who aren't afraid to start meditation cannot imagine why anyone would. But I have encountered many artists who are afraid, if not terrified, thinking they will literally go mad, turn into some kind of mindless vegetable, or even become a member of some cult. They might think that the inherently pacifying qualities of meditation will extinguish creative inspiration. And deep down, some artists fear that if meditation fosters insight, they might discover that they are wasting time trying to be a creative person. Even if you aren't afraid of meditation these are important points that need to be addressed.

Fear of meditation is based on deeper fears of change and discovery. As creative people, we wouldn't imagine this would be an issue, since creativity has everything to do with discovery and change. If you are an art-maker, at some point you rebelled against something in order to be original. You likely experienced this as a fundamental act of bravery. And yet, deep down inside, there is one thing we are afraid to mess with: our creative process. Even though we may have read or heard about how people have benefited from meditation, we fear it will not work for us because—as art-makers—we see ourselves as different from others.

As creative people, at one time or another, to one degree or another, we have come to feel that we have glimpsed the world in a way that few others have. We tend not to speak of this, but it is an open secret. Most people have also had such a glimpse, but as art-makers it has become the foundation of our vocation or avocation. This glimpse has left many of us with not only a source of inspiration but also a means to our creative process. However, it is a means that we have a tenuous connection to and very little control over. This can lead to all sorts of doubts about self-confidence and whether our process is real or imagined.

If we harbor such doubts, any technique such as meditation—which leads us repeatedly back to our own minds, thoughts, and emotions—can scare the hell out of us. What if we are the type of person who has worked very hard to suppress certain things and we fear that if we meditate, if we give ourselves sufficient space, we might not be able to keep them down any longer? And we might then lose whatever control over our process that we once had. On the opposite side, we might feel that the whole reason we are creative is because what is buried in us is constantly erupting. If we meditate, it might all dissolve and cause us to lose our edge, our motivation, our source of material. Or we might suddenly discover we have brainwashed ourselves into thinking we are creative people when we are actually not.

I hear all of this a great deal, but after more than thirty-five years of meditating and teaching meditation, I have not seen anyone quit being creative because they took up the practice of meditation. I have seen people change. I have seen their work change. I have even seen people take a break for a while, but never have I seen anyone give up their passion to discover and create. It seems locked into our very being as if it were part of our genetic code.

I have found it easier to encourage a logical, linear, left-brained individual to practice meditation than a creative, intuitive, right-brained individual. This is because creative people often believe that their process is the same as formal meditation. So they see meditation as a waste of time. No matter how contemplative one's creative process is, it is simply not the same as formal meditation practice. At its best, our creative process can be what is called "meditation-in-action." But without the mental and physical stillness found in meditation, there is always some kind of movement, some subtle goal to produce something within our creative process. In formal meditation, we have space to experience ourselves beyond our impulses—to create, to destroy, to manipulate, to alter, even to better something. Meditation-in-action, or creative process, is a wonderful byproduct of this formal meditation practice.

Where We Rest Our Minds

By practicing meditation, we work directly with the nature of our minds and our experiences in a process of exploration and discovery. This becomes the basis for understanding, appreciating, and manifesting all other activities with mindfulness and awareness. Meditation makes the most of our mind's natural ability to rest on an object. The mind naturally comes to rest on whatever it perceives or is directed toward. It can rest on our creative process, which is desirable, but it can also rest on distractions such as our hopes and fears, TV, radio, past or present arguments, memories, sounds, or a tragedy in our life. Basically, it can rest on whatever comes into our mind or senses: good or bad.

Meditation is essentially neutral, and it offers us the chance to be goalless. By choosing the object of meditation and establishing the view of the practice itself, we can meditate on things that will make us feel better or worse, things that make us angry or appreciative, and things that will put us to sleep or wake us up. While we can even use meditation to reinforce prejudices, ego, passion, aggression, or for that matter withdrawal from the world altogether, meditation has the power to break down prejudices, calm incessant self-dialoging, and become a powerful tool for discovery and play. It can lead us toward a more expansive and inclusive vision, and a wakeful, energetic, unselfconscious creative process that transcends culture and time. It's really up to us to choose what we wish to rest our mind on as well as whether we wish to put ourselves to sleep or wake ourselves up.

Chapter Two

The Importance of Doing Nothing

For thousands of years, humanity has been telling stories that describe the beneficial effects of meditation. Today there is also significant scientific data supporting those anecdotes, some of which has been published in popular books and mainstream magazines. We know that meditation, at minimum, can reduce anxiety, stress, and blood pressure. Even an inexperienced practitioner of meditation can taste such effects after several sessions. There have been brain scans of seasoned meditators showing that the prefrontal cortex, which is concerned with orientation and awareness, becomes more active while the parietal lobe, which is concerned with self-referencing, quiets down. All totaled, meditation leads to a sense of oneness, wholeness, or unity with nature, humanity, or with one's sense of the divine.[1] If a meditator has a dedicated practice under the guidance of an experienced teacher, meditation can have a positive transformative effect on every aspect of his or her life.

Doing Nothing Properly

One of the goals embedded in all mindfulness meditation practices is "to see things as they are." As art-makers we all too frequently and painfully experience a vast gap between our inspiration and what we communicate. The ability to glimpse things as they are—as opposed to how we think, hope, or fear they are—provides a precious tool in the creative process. It offers the opportunity to take the clarity we perceive and transform it into the result we desire, which will in turn communicate what we wish.

Perceiving things as they are leads to perceiving ourselves as we are. This in turn helps us to know the difference between *self-expression*, which can be fraught with self-consciousness, awkwardness, hesitation, and self-doubt, and *pure expression*, which is not so afflicted.

There is such a thing as unconditional expression that does not come from self or other. It manifests out of nowhere like mushrooms in a meadow, like hailstones, like thundershowers.

~ *Chögyam Trungpa Rinpoche* [2]

The path toward perceiving things as they are and better defining our creative process begins with learning how to do nothing properly. We might argue that we have already mastered this skill because we often find ourselves doing nothing when waiting for something or stuck in traffic, after an unsuccessful day in the studio or a futile day spent reading nonsense on a computer screen.

When we think we are doing nothing, are we *really* doing nothing? At minimum, we could find ourselves busy being guilty about doing nothing and stressing about what we should or could be doing. Even if we are physically doing very little, our minds are actively recalling something, pursuing something, planning, worrying, or self-dialoguing about something. In such moments, we are actually making something out of the nothing we think we have.

There is a point to doing truly nothing—to arrive at a state of mind so spacious that something fresh and original can arise and be recognized. When we start to draw or paint, we start with a blank surface. If we begin a dance, we start with an empty stage. At the beginning of a creative project, we generally commence with a physical space that is empty rather than full. But our state of mind doesn't follow this practice. We start with a mind that is already filled with thoughts, storylines, plans, concepts, emotions, pains, pleasures, and on and on. It's as though our mind is a stage overfilled with actors, dancers, performers, stage hands, and business managers all bumping into one another, carrying on conversations and arguments. And some are trying to stretch and twirl and do whatever is their job, discipline, or craft. With minds so full, we push forward expecting to invent and create a great performance.

In truth, as we reach to create from this space, we are mining for more thoughts, more conversations or arguments; as they surface we collect them and cram them into the already crowded stage in our heads. And, as if that is not sufficient, we inject some caffeine or the like, surround it with the stress of self-consciousness, a good measure of hope and fear, shake it all up, and expect some gems to pop out like golden eggs from a goose. Under such circumstances it's a miracle when anything of interest happens. If this were an actual scenario on a stage, it would seem obvious that we first need to quiet the voices, calm the activity, and get everyone's attention, as well as let go of some of the individuals who don't need to be there. The same logic should be applied to our minds.

On one hand, we tell ourselves to "slow down and smell the roses," but for most of us, if the roses get in the way of our creative process they get ignored at best and trampled at worst. Many of us have grown up with the saying "Idle hands are the devil's tools." We feel we have to be doing something not only to be a "good" person, but to feel we exist at all. Some of us so identify with our thoughts that we feel if we're not thinking, we don't exist.

One cognitive study showed that about a quarter of the time, we are actually not thinking about anything. What meditators refer to as moments of "nonthought" just happen without even trying. When the subjects of the study were told this result, most refused to believe that they were not thinking all the time. Even after given proof, they still challenged it.[3]

On one hand, when we are meditating we are doing something: we are practicing. We are practicing the discipline of doing nothing properly. That might sound like a contradiction or a Japanese koan meant to boggle conceptual mind,[4] but it means that during the practice of meditation, we drop everything except for the technique itself, even the notion that we are doing something really helpful and important. We have to let it go.

Letting Go

Letting something go is not suppression. It is not ignoring anything, either. We could say that when a thought comes up it is like a limousine that arrives at our front door and is there to take us to a place we would really like to go, where we feel drawn. But we do not have to get in and go for the ride. If we don't, and simply continue to practice, it will drive off on its own. It might not be long before another arrives, but we don't have to take that one either. If we get into the limousine, no matter how seductive the vehicle or how quiet and smooth the ride, it is ultimately taking us away from being in the moment, where we are awake, aware, and more fully present. As we will see, meditation practice develops a mindfulness and awareness that leaks into our creative and viewing processes as well as our whole lives. Meditation is not something extraordinary or necessarily difficult, but simply a process of returning the mind to the present moment whenever it drifts off. With practice, we can all do that. What is challenging is relaxing, thought by thought, all the conditioning that steals us away from appreciating who we are and where we are. Among the many benefits of learning to let go and do nothing properly, as done in meditation, is the discovery of a vital tool for the creative process: the ability to glimpse things as they truly are.

Figure 1: *"A Dot in Space" by Chögyam Trungpa Rinpoche,*
referring to the birth of inspiration

Chapter Three

Meditation Instruction

Meditation instruction is best when it is individualized. It's fine to get started with the instructions offered here. But, things can be interpreted differently. Little misunderstandings can happen and, as intelligent beings, we have an amazing ability to deceive ourselves even with a practice that is designed to cut through self-deception. Therefore, it is advisable to find and develop a relationship with an experienced meditation instructor. In this case, someone who is experienced with mindfulness and awareness practice; also known as *shamatha* and *vipassana*, which can be translated as "calm abiding" and "insight" meditation. An experienced instructor also knows how to tweak the practice to fit an individual's personality and ability.

Holding the View

Practicing meditation without a view is like waiting for something to appear without any means of recognizing it when it shows up. Having a thorough understanding of the view empowers our practice. It also helps us to appreciate the results we attain.

The practice and the view work hand in hand. The view encompasses an understanding of the practice and its purpose. Whereas the mechanics of the practice might change little over time, the view usually expands and matures as time goes by.

Much of what is shared in this book is the view of the practices we engage in.

To begin with, we are not using meditation to ignore personal issues, withdraw from the world, achieve some altered or higher mental state, or solve a problem. We are trying to do our best to have a sense of stillness while being awake and aware of whatever is happening. The byproduct of this nonactivity is the ability to glimpse things as they are: unfiltered and undistorted. When some stability is achieved in the formal practice, it naturally expands to what is called meditation-in-action, which encompasses our creative and viewing processes.

These meditation instructions are nonreligious; in fact they are said to predate the major religions. Being nontheistic, a belief system is unnecessary, and sometimes even a distraction. You don't even need to believe meditation practice will work.

If you have practiced some forms of Buddhist meditation, the following instructions will be familiar. Buddhism has handed these instructions down for thousands of years in the way they were received. While studying Buddhist philosophy and psychology will deepen your understanding and view of this practice, it will not make the practice itself any easier to do.

Although these instructions are simple, they have depth and subtlety, and it will take several pages to share them. Remember that ultimately, we are trying to do less, rather than more. You can grow into this practice. It is the basis and backbone for many other meditative and contemplative practices and one that most practitioners continue to do throughout their entire lives. It serves to keep us connected to our art-making and -viewing.

Working with the Body

Let's begin with posture. You will need a comfortable place to sit, but not so comfortable that you lounge or slouch. The goal is to sit so that your breathing is unrestricted and you won't simply fall asleep. The reason meditators typically sit upright on a cushion arranged on the floor with their legs crossed is because this position offers the best posture to meet the goal. When sitting this way, it's difficult to fall asleep without falling over.

Meditation is not a test of your physical fitness or your ability to endure pain. If you cannot sit in this fashion there are other ways to have a good posture. For example, you can sit on a firm cushion. Your knees should not touch the floor when your legs are crossed but you will likely be more comfortable if your knees are below the level of your hips. If you have a meditation bench and like it, use it. If you need to sit in a chair, do so, but it should not encourage you to lean back into it and fall asleep. It is also important to not slump forward, which will restrict breathing. A good chair will encourage you to remain upright, but not stiff. In general, you should avoid leaning against things for support. The goal here is to have a posture that fosters a sense of alert relaxation.

If you become really uncomfortable, you can gently and subtly shift your position and continue practicing. But not every little twitch and itch and little discomfort requires relief. As you will come to see, these instructions are all about achieving balance in which we are not being too rigid or too casual. By taking this posture, we are working with our mind and body and their connection to one another. It is useful to see the posture we take as giving shape to our mind. For example, when our bodies are slumped over, our minds are slumped. Our bodies reflect our state of mind and having a good supportive posture enhances our practice.

Keep your eyes open and relaxed. Although the eyes are open, they are not especially focused on anything in particular. Let them rest on an open space about three to six feet in front. The gaze should feel comfortable and yet not resting on anything in particular nor searching for anything. Keeping your eyes open helps us to mix our mind with the environment and develop awareness as well as mindfulness. If you close your eyes, there is a greater likelihood that you will fall asleep, drift off into some fantasy, or get involved in a lot of self-dialoguing. Meditating with the eyes open is especially helpful with the creative processes, in that you are learning how to bring as many senses—if not all of them—into your practice and from there bring your mindfulness and awareness practice into your process. If it has been a particularly challenging day, you may need to close your eyes to get settled in. In that case, close your eyes until you are ready to try opening them.

After you become experienced with meditation, you might find yourself naturally raising your gaze a bit and that is OK. However, if you find yourself looking around at things, then bring yourself back by returning to a lower gaze.

Breath as the Object of Attention

The object of this meditation is our breath. We gently focus on the breath because it is something we can rest our minds on, but it cannot be held on to physically or psychologically. We direct our attention to the breath as it rises and falls, as the air goes in and out. Even though we could control it to a degree, we shouldn't. It happens on its own and we let it. We only need to be aware of it. Anything we do to manipulate the breath only takes us away from our goal of doing nothing.

When we practice resting our mind on our breath, we are training our mind to be where we place it. Because the breath is a neutral activity and happens on its own, it offers a simple means to ground our mind in our body and in the space they are in, rather than encourage us to fantasize about the future or worry about the past. When we follow our breath, we develop mindfulness, in which our minds are filled with the object of meditation. When some stability is achieved with the practice, the byproduct of mindfulness practice is a wakeful awareness of the breath and the environment as a whole.

This meditation practice is not about concentration. It is about opening up, tuning in, and being more inclusive and sensitive. During the process of resting our mind on the breath, we may notice a slight difference between our in-breath, with the air coming in, and the out-breath, with the air going out. The in-breath, in a sense, fills us up and the out-breath has a quality of dissolving as it goes out and mixes with the air in the environment. As our attention follows the breath out, there is a sensation that we are going out with it and also mixing with the environment. The out-breath actually takes a bit longer than the in-breath. This observation can be helpful to us. This slight imbalance can encourage us to let go more than hold on. Mindfulness of the sensation of going out with the out-breath leads us to be less self-conscious and less self-referential, and encourages the development of awareness. This slight difference extends our mindfulness of the breath to include the environment. If you find yourself thinking too much about this subtle difference between the in- and the out-breath, you should just let go of any distinction between the two. Once you settle into meditation practice, you can explore it again.

Sometimes beginners, as well as experienced practitioners, have difficulty following the breath at all and find it helpful to count the breaths. An in- and out-breath would be counted as one. When you count to ten, return to one. When you drift off and forget which number you are on—and you will—don't try to remember, just start over at one. We are not accumulating numbers but practicing mindfulness.

By attending to the breath, we are also learning to synchronize our mind with our body so they are in the same place at the same time. In other words, our mind is not off daydreaming about being one place while our body is in another. It is when our mind and body are synchronized that we are in our natural state.

Working with Thoughts

Thoughts incessantly pop up and turn into thought streams that feed self-dialoguing, which in turn can explode into emotional upheaval. This happens in life as well as in meditation, only in meditation it is more obvious. After several minutes of practice, we may have lost the breath and all sense of what we are doing. While we might think that we have failed—after all, isn't meditation about not thinking?—we are in fact practicing correctly. Meditation trains us to recognize when we have completely drifted off from our experience and how we can to return to it. If we never drifted off, we would not need to meditate.

Meditation is not about becoming thoughtless, mindless, and without emotions. It is not a discipline of thought suppression or thought manipulation. It is the practice of returning the mind to its natural resting state in which it is not ruled by thoughts and emotions. So when we realize we have been absorbed in thought, we can see it as just another opportunity to simply relax and return our attention to the breath.

Spacious Mind and the Creative Process

When we meditate, we begin to surround our thoughts with space and that space offers perspective. We have glimpses of clarity, wakefulness, peace, and a greater sense of aliveness. It has been said that before we meditate our minds are like a perpetually cloud-covered sky and we have come to mistake the clouds for the sky. When we begin to meditate, we see cracks in the cloud covering and as blue sky appears, we begin to see that our thoughts and emotions are not all there is. It might even scare us. As the cloud cover separates into individual clouds, we experience the bright blue sky as well as the intense light and heat of the sun, which clearly illuminates all it touches. We can no longer be fooled into thinking that there are only clouds. In the same way, our thoughts lose their tight grip on us. We can see beyond them and their presence or absence no longer distracts us from the truth of things as they are.

The spaciousness found in meditation also allows the possibility of thoughts to arise and naturally dissolve in a way that does not immediately lead to another thought stream or an emotional upheaval. Because of this spaciousness, there is room for something different, new, and original to arise. We might like or dislike what arises, but at this stage it is important to not get caught up in or latch onto it, but to return to our practice of minding the breath.

As creative people, we can readily get caught up in trying to develop an inspiration that arises during meditation, or for that matter, mine what floats to the surface for some storyline. After all, why are we doing this if we can't take advantage of such moments? You can, but now is not the time. If we are lying in wait to pounce on whatever inspiration arises, we are not really meditating. We are a spider waiting for prey.

In some ways, meditation is like having an investment account. If we immediately spend every dividend we accumulate, our account never grows. Our investment in meditation accumulates space, a sense of environment, and a deeper relationship to our senses. In order to do that, we have to let go of whatever arises: the good stuff as well as the bad. We see it as it arises, in a sense we acknowledge it by not ignoring it, and then we let it go.

Having said that, if an irresistible creative thought arises and the only way to get your mind back to the breath is to briefly write something down, then do it quickly and gently and return to the practice. You will come to trust that it's unnecessary—the truly relevant inspirations do come back to you after the session is over.

Labeling Thoughts "Thinking"

Often we need help letting go of our thoughts. When we spontaneously realize we are thinking rather than following our breath, we can label our thoughts, thought streams, and even emotions all as "thinking." It is easier to return to the breath after we acknowledge the thoughts by mentally saying "thinking." This action provides closure to the thought stream without suppressing or crushing it. It also short circuits the self-criticism that can occur when we discover we have drifted off from meditation practice. Self-criticism is just another thought stream that you can label. The objective here is to put a period at the end of our thoughts and gently come back to following our breath without creating a firestorm of additional thoughts.

In the beginning, it may seem that we spend most of our time caught up in thoughts and rarely remember to follow our breath. However, the more we practice, the more we shift toward being present with our breath and the environment. Even the need to label thoughts as "thinking" begins to drift away. In this way, we are training our minds to be present, to rest on what we want it to, when we want it to.

Meditating with Emotions

Emotions are thoughts with rocket boosters attached to them. They have an enormous amount of energy and history to fuel them on their way. When emotions arise during meditation practice, we treat them as thoughts and label them "thinking."

Emotions can be daunting to work with during meditation. They come with such force that even labeling can seem futile. Some practitioners feel they just can't do it and even stop meditating. As I have said, meditation is a neutral, open ground. It doesn't suppress or foster emotions. If you have suppressed a great deal of personal business for a long time and you suddenly stop doing that, then it appears as if meditation is encouraging those emotions and the resulting chaos to arise. The art of meditating with emotions is to simply let things find their own balance, but until they do, it can feel as if things are out of control. Meditation is a workable environment to face many emotions. When emotions are met with sufficient space and gentleness, they tend to self-dissolve just as thoughts do. At the same time, meditation is by no means a substitute for therapy if therapy is needed. For some of us, conventional therapy would achieve better results, particularly with extreme emotions. A credentialed therapist with a significant background in meditation can be very supportive. In addition, just as thoughts never entirely cease during meditation, neither do emotions. As you develop your practice, you will not feel things less. If anything, meditation will make you feel more deeply, empathetically, and compassionately toward yourself and others.

Duration and Frequency

How long and often to meditate? Any length of time meditating, no matter how short, is better than not meditating. Even two minutes will help, but it will merely contribute some fresh air to the mind whereas with twenty minutes there is at least a chance of settling in with your breath. Forty minutes is better than twenty. Cognitive science supports this with its discovery of what meditators have known for centuries: it takes about forty minutes for the average mind to settle down and get bored. Although the purpose of meditation is not to bore you, or for that matter entertain you, boredom is a sign post and is a good thing. More inspiration seems to occur out of the space of boredom than from intense multitasking. Boredom is a sign that we have run out of distractions—it means our mind is settling down and beginning to synchronize with our body and the environment. Not much is happening except for irritation.

As we become more experienced practitioners, the irritation transforms into stability. If we can sit for an hour, we often get a taste of that stability. Toward the end of that period of time, the average meditator is more likely to be meditating than trying to meditate, and more likely to be experiencing the present moment, rather than remembering the past or imagining the future. This is the fundamental purpose of meditation: to learn not only how to be here now more often than not, but also to be mindful of it.

It is recommended that you practice in the morning before you get caught up in your daily routine. It can be a challenge to settle into your practice at the end of the day. The momentum of the events that have transpired can carry into your practice. Practicing in the morning *and* evening is especially good for developing overall stability in your meditation practice.

As we develop mindfulness, we establish an environment for the arising of awareness and the birth of insight and inspiration. Awareness, insight, and inspiration cannot be directly hunted down and caught—it is more likely that "if you build it, they will come." Mindfulness practice is the building of an environment that invites awareness, insight, and inspiration, and it is mindfulness that allows us to play with them once they arrive.

Chapter Four

Perception Is More Important Than Talent

*Without seeing things as they are, it is hard to
create art. Our perceptions are obscured and our mind is not
fresh, so making art becomes a troubled, futile process by
which we're trying to create something based on concept.*

~ Sakyong Mipham Rinpoche[1]

Without clarity of perception, whatever talent we have only has an accidental chance of being skillfully applied. Have you ever worked on a project and showed it to a fresh set of eyes only to discover it is not anything like you thought it was? If we perceive things entirely through the filters of our thoughts, hopes, and fears, and then try to make art, we are working with our projections rather than things as they are. If we cannot perceive things as they are, how can we possibly work with our projects as they are or perceive our results for what they are?

Meditation offers a clarity that helps us to see through our thoughts and emotions to things as they are. It assists us in applying our existing skills and facilitates the learning of new ones. For example, drawing is a skill. Drawing teachers know that anyone can be taught the basics. In the beginning, they do not teach the skill of drawing—rather they teach how to perceive the object to be drawn. They also teach how to see the results and compare them to the object. The student's skills flow from proper perception.

Many beginners reproduce what they *think* they are looking at rather than what they actually *perceive*. If a class is given a rectangular table to draw and they have never attempted it before, invariably there will be students who know conceptually that the table is composed of rectangular shapes. From that they will infer that the goal is to draw rectangular shapes to represent the table, such as in the example below.

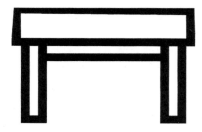

Figure 2: *Square Table*

However, the result does not look quite right. It "thinks" right in that it possesses rectangular shapes. But if the student studies the object more closely, they notice that because they are standing at an angle to the table, very little of the table is actually rectangular. When a student attempts to draw what they actually observe, the results look more like the following example, which includes visual perspective.

Figure 3: *Square Table in Perspective*

From a two-dimensional point of view, the tabletop is a trapezoid and not a rectangle. Viewed from another angle, it would be something else. In fact, all the shapes would change. If we do not have the clarity of perception to perceive this, then we cannot accurately reproduce it. While drawing is much more than accurately reproducing something because it involves style and expression, our clarity of perception increases our ability to achieve our desired result. And meditation practice facilitates this clarity of perception.

Meditation Leads to Meditation-in-Action

The more we practice meditation, the more we become aware of what is called the "post-meditation" experience, which occurs after our formal practice is finished. The clarity, wakefulness, and awareness that have developed during a practice session seem to continue for a period of time afterward. The more we practice, the longer the post-meditation experience lingers.

This is different from what is called "meditation-in-action." Meditation-in-action is when we bring the same discipline of mindfulness and awareness practice to whatever we are doing: creative process, viewing process, or any everyday life activity. For example, if we are engaged in drawing and wish to engage mindfulness practice as we work, we could do so by using the thing we are drawing as the object of meditation rather than the breath. In doing so, we observe and appreciate more of what we are drawing. This allows us to be as faithful to the object as we wish. We might even choose not to be faithful; we might even create an abstraction. But in either case, the result will be based on the clarity of our perception.

Meditation-in-action is not limited to being mindful of one object or activity. It can include our entire creative process, and more. Formal meditation practice leads to the post-meditation experience, which in turn leads to confidence in our practice. From there we begin to discover that we can bring mindfulness and our awareness to all kinds of activities. That is when life itself becomes an endless source of inspiration, discovery, and play.

Misperceptions

Formal meditation or meditation-in-action can help us perceive our world better, but is not a cure-all for misperceptions. Some misperceptions are due to the limitations of our sense perceptions. Rita Carter, in her book *Exploring Consciousness*, points out that even when we think we have clear, detailed perceptions they are incomplete. This happens because the brain synthesizes any missing parts to complete a picture in order to make a more rational world.

*Within-the-moment visual consciousness is ... limited to a
handful of clear perceptions, and the apparent detail is an
illusion ... Our impoverished visual perceptions are fleshed out
by our memories of the perceptions that went before, and our
expectations of what will come next.*

~ *Rita Carter,* Exploring Consciousness[2]

Cognitive science and neuroscience have discovered that our
brains attempt to make educated guesses and sometimes fail to
get it right. Until recently, eyewitness identification has been the
primary method used to solve criminal cases. The Justice Project
has stated that the leading cause of wrongful conviction is eyewitness misidentification.

Magicians and illusionists make successful careers out of
how faulty our perceptions are and how suggestive our minds
can be. *Scientific American Mind* magazine recently reported that
neuroscientists met with magicians in order to learn more about
how magicians exploit loopholes in the brain's circuitry.[3]

Our perceptions and misperceptions also provide subject
matter for artists. In 1754, William Hogarth created a work that
played with our perception of scale and perspective in his painting
False Perspective. He drew people and animals in the background
the same size as others were in the middle ground, confusing our
perception of their position in space. Upon viewing, our brains try
to arrive at a complete and rational picture—only to be confounded
by the placement and size. Our brain naturally attempts to switch
to another view, only to arrive at yet another visual contradiction.

Baroque faux-painted ceilings in the 1600s give the illusion of
vast space. Some say that the Cubist movement is based on the realization that the three-dimensional vision we experience is created

in our brain from what is actually a two-dimensional perception. In a way, many Cubist paintings capture a three-dimensional world crushed like a pack of cigarettes in a two-dimensional object. The Dutch artist M. C. Escher created ambiguous renderings of stairs, buildings, and nature. Salvador Dali is known for his work with the ambiguous figures seen in *Voltaire–Slave Market* in which the two central figures, their dress, and the doorway combine to form the face of Voltaire. The Op Art Movement of the 1960s took perceptual issues to the extreme. Hans Holbein (1497–1543) preceded that movement by several hundred years with *The Ambassadors*. In this painting, there appears to be a smear at the feet of the ambassadors. But when viewed at an extremely oblique angle, the smear appears as a normal rendering of a skull.

If you wish to explore further the inherent weaknesses of our perceptions, you only need to visit one of the many websites or books devoted to optical illusions. Here is one that is called an "ambiguous figure," composed of a series of lines and circles. At first glance it appears as a three-dimensional trident. But on further examination, we notice that the lines do not line up the way they should.

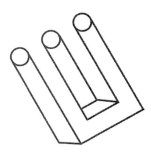

Figure 4: *Ambiguous Trident*

It is actually quite uncomfortable to look at this figure for any length of time as our brain struggles to rationalize its shape. According to neuroscience, what is happening when we are confronted with such visual imagery is that each side of the brain is taking in the information differently and constructing its own view of reality. Each side of the brain then competes for supremacy. It's called "interhemispheric switching" and we experience it as a perceptual waffling.[4] Experiments have shown that laughter temporarily rebalances and synchronizes both halves of the brain so that the two views blend into one for a period of time.

This is also true for meditation. Medical studies have uncovered that the synchronization of mind and body that occurs through chanting, prayer, contemplation, and meditation lowers heart rate, blood pressure, and breathing rate—all of which contribute to health and well-being. But while meditation will not extend the abilities of our sense perceptions beyond their capacities, it will help to dissolve any extraneous influences on our perceptions so they may resynchronize with each other, resulting in a more accurate view.

Our brains also demand constancy and when it is not offered, it will attempt to manufacture it. There are many types of constancy, such as shape constancy, color constancy, contrast and brightness constancy. The brain divides up the sensory information it receives and deposits it in various locations based on the type of information. When the brain recalls perceptions and something is missing, or seems not right, it struggles to make it right.

We can experience this first hand when viewing Rene Magritte's *Les Valeurs Personnelles* (*Personal Values*), 1952.

The painting displays ordinary objects out of proportion to their size against a wall made of sky: unsettling imagery. He plays with our brain's need for size constancy. If it were just one object that was out of place or the wrong size, our brains might find some compromised view and settle down. But because so many objects are out of constancy, our perceptions jump from one object to another as if our mind cannot find any place to rest. The effort of the artist, architect, or designer to make things "look right" is frequently a battle to achieve constancy.

What We Miss with Familiarity

Familiarity with objects can profoundly dull our perceptions. Try this simple contemplative exercise: before entering a familiar room, take a pad and pen and—without peeking into that room—write down what you recall about it. Take a minute or two. Then enter the room and stand in the center of it. Your task is to make one slow, 360-degree turn that takes twenty minutes to complete.

Don't panic—you have spent at least twenty minutes doing far more ridiculous things than this. While making this rotation, keep your eyes open and in front as you turn. Keep all your senses open and breathe normally. Don't answer the phone or the door, and if you have others in the household let them know what you are going to be doing so they don't bother you. At first, you might imagine that this is a terribly long time and want to speed it up or cut it short. Please don't—you will have a different opinion about the time afterward. You can wear a watch and check it to see how you are doing. At each quarter of the turn, which is ninety degrees, five minutes should have elapsed. If you are not precisely there, you don't have to correct your position, but merely adjust your pace.

Now stop reading and do this. If you don't stop reading now and end up doing the rotation after reading what follows, you will always wonder if you were talked into the experience.

After completing the rotation, pick up your paper and pen and *without* looking around, take a minute or two to write down whatever you now recall about the room. Next, compare what you first wrote with what you now wrote. Reading it out loud is helpful. What's different about each list? After the rotation, you probably noticed things you never noticed before and found things you forgot were there. Ask yourself if there is a qualitative difference in the second list. Did the same things catch your attention? Was it all visual or did you engage any of your other senses? Although there are no right answers, I find most people not only discover that they saw much more of their environment than they had for some time, but also heard, smelled, and felt more during the rotation. Also, when they read their two lists, they tend to find the second list more experiential and even somewhat poetic. Many find that the twenty minutes they spent doing the exercise was not such a long time after all.

Why is it that so much in our familiar environment is not experienced? Have we found ourselves looking for inspiration everywhere but where we are? In contrast, there are numerous artists, writers, and musicians who find some of their greatest inspirations in their room, house, garden, and on the street where they live.

Objectivity of Our Subjectivity

In addition to the inherent weaknesses of our perceptions, our thoughts also affect our perceptions. If you need some convincing, try this thought experiment. Think about the saliva in your mouth and how clean, lubricating, and fresh it is. Take a moment to experience it. Now, if you collected some of it in a cup and then examined it, what would you now think of it? Would you still perceive it to be clean and fresh? Would you consider drinking it? Probably not! The thought of it would likely be disgusting even though merely seconds before it was in your mouth where you are constantly swallowing it. How is it possible that our perceptions of the same thing could be so radically different only seconds apart? Whether we find a hair in our dinner and lose our appetite or hear someone say something that completely changes our perception of them, our thoughts have changed our perceptions. In these two examples, we did find a hair and did hear what was said; but what about all the times when we were not paying full attention and we thought we saw or heard something only to find out that we didn't see it or hear it accurately after we had acted on it?

> *Nobody today is normal, everybody is a little bit crazy or unbalanced, people's minds are running all the time. Their perceptions of the world are partial, incomplete. They are eaten alive by their egos. They think they see, but they are mistaken; all they do is project their madness, their world, upon the world. There is no clarity, no wisdom in that!*
>
> ~ *Taisen Deshimaru (1914-1982)* [5]

Is there a remedy? Is it possible to reduce the influence our thoughts, prejudices, and biases have on our perceptions? Can we ever be completely sure we are seeing things totally as they are? If our thoughts can so readily affect our perceptions then it would seem that our idealized notion of objectivity is not possible because it would always be colored by the possibility of some error or subjectivity. Meditative disciplines say it is possible to have perceptions that are not obscured by our thoughts without becoming bland like some objective scientific instrument.

We can attain a state of objective subjectivity. In other words, we can be objective about our own subjectivity. We learn to see our subjectivity for what it is and to be objective about our filters and limitations. We can also work to obtain a fuller and more accurate picture of what is going on, whether it is within our creative process or the world around us. We do this by learning how to synchronize our mind and body and resting all our senses on whatever is taking place. Objective subjectivity is achievable with the assistance of meditation. It even brings the experience of seeing through our subjectivity. After all, to even acknowledge that we are subjective means we must have glimpsed something beyond it.

There is a side benefit to realizing that our perceptions are not nearly as complete and unbiased as we would like to think. We become less dogmatic in asserting our views and more welcoming of those from others. When other peoples' perceptions seem contrary to ours, it is actually an opportunity to gather additional information and fill in the gaps of our own perceptions. All of this can lead toward a more complete view of ourselves and others, which makes us more compassionate.

Chapter Five

Felt Sense and Thought Sense

The truth of the thing is not the think of it but the feel of it.
~ Stanley Kubrick[1]

One eye sees, the other feels.
~ Paul Klee[2]

B efore I can share more specifics about how meditation can benefit the creative and viewing processes, I need to further define the nature of experience from the point of view of meditation. It is also important to note that the viewing process is not limited to sight, but includes, to a degree, the other senses. In some instances, sight will take a lesser role—in a musical performance, sound is the predominant sense in the "viewing" process.

Let us start the exploration of our experience with the two uses of the word "sense."

Felt Sense

Fundamentally, our experience consists of sensing things—as in perceiving them, and then making sense of them—as in knowing them. Sensing involves multiple perceptions working in conjunction, whether we are conscious of them individually or not. The immediate result of perceiving things is a sensation that is frequently referred to as a gut feeling, gut sense, intuitive sense, or felt sense. Whatever the label, it is a direct experience that occurs either before or without conceptualization or ratiocination. It is prelanguage. It is a type of knowing that is not encumbered by a thought stream. Timothy D. Wilson, in his book *Strangers to Ourselves*,[3] refers to this type of knowing as the "adaptive unconscious." In Buddhist psychology, it is the moment when all our senses are engaged in some fashion and working in concert, but without self-consciousness or self-dialoguing. This is part of what is meant by "seeing things as they are," as opposed to merely seeing them according to how we think they are. We often have this experience when we come across something for the first time and don't yet know what it is. It could be described as an "Oh!" moment. We are surprised, curious, engaged, and we might utter, "Oh, what's this?" Our experience of it at that moment consists of a felt sense.

Thought Sense

When we discover what the object is, we have a thought sense of it. Our "Oh!" moment transforms in to an "Ah-ha!" The thought sense can involve labeling, comparing, categorizing, and self-dialoguing about the object as a way to make "sense" of it, to know it. Guy Claxton, author of *Hare Brain, Tortoise Mind: Why Intelligence Increases When You Think Less*,[4] calls this thought sense, "deliberative mode" or "D-mode."

A thought sense in Buddhist psychology begins when the five senses are engaged and their individual experiences are brought together in our mind[5] (which is considered a sixth sense) where they are turned into a coherent experience that has the potential to rise to the level of consciousness. If it does rise to the level of consciousness, it generally turns into a thought. There are many experiences that do not rise to the level of consciousness. Think of all the bug bites you have had and how many of them you were conscious of during the moment of attack. What about all the sounds we hear that go unnoticed unless we stop to listen? We have many more felt senses than thought senses. It doesn't seem so to us because we are so often caught up in thoughts about thoughts rather than our immediate experience. Therefore, many of our felt senses go completely unnoticed.

Imagine you are walking in a rose garden and find you have the time to smell the roses. The sight of the rose, the scent of the rose, the sound of bees humming as they collect their nectar, the wind brushing against our skin and rustling the leaves—all assemble in our mind to form as complete an experience of the rose as possible. The next step, turning the felt sense into a thought sense, takes place so quickly that we are unaware that multiple things took place: felt and thought senses. We so often become so caught up in our thought sense that we start thinking about our thoughts: *It's a rose; what kind of rose it is; would it make a nice bouquet; oops, I forgot my anniversary; oh no, what can I do about it; is there a florist nearby; what time is it, etc.* All further separating us from the original sensation and experience.

Thought Sense Can Make Sense

Not all thought senses end up inspiring thought streams that completely remove us from our original experience. Some take us back to the experience or lead us to a new experience or discovery, and increased knowledge or wisdom. One example is the act of labeling a thought stream "thinking" during meditation.

In meditation, we start with placing our attention on the breath and we experience our own breathing—the felt sense of the rhythm of the breath. At some point, often much too quickly, we drift off from that felt sense into a thought stream and, in a way, we are gone. Sometime later, often not soon enough, something calls us back or wakes us up to the fact that we have lost contact with being present with our experience. It is usually our body. We experience an itch, or ache, or sound, or some movement—something that cuts through our stream of thoughts and abruptly our mind is back in our bodies. The thought sense that suddenly arises from that experience is usually something like, "Oh no! I am not following my breath." That thought sense causes us to invoke the instruction to label our thoughts as "thinking" in order to help us come back to the felt sense of our breathing. In this way, meditation is a process of learning to recognize when we have drifted off from our experience and how we can to return to it decisively and with gentleness. It also teaches us that our thought sense can and does have an important role, particularly when it is connected to, or directing us toward, an experience.

Our thought sense naturally follows our felt sense when it is allowed to. There is a certain sanity connected to this order. If we touch something that is hot, we feel the heat and immediately think, "Hot!" If we have not recently touched something hot and try to think "hot," we would likely come up with only a fantasy of the experience. In fact, knowing something is hot before we touch it may only serve to heighten our senses because we are still surprised by how it feels. The thought of an experience is just not the same as the experience. But, there is no reason for them to be the same because they play separate and complementary roles.

While our thought sense naturally comes second, it does not mean it is secondary. The mind can know things that are not knowable by sensory experience, such as abstract thoughts and ideas, which are also vital to us and without which we would have no idea what is written on this page or any other. After all, a sense, such as sight, only sees what it sees. When the thought sense of things comes about through the direct sensory experience of things, aka felt sense, it is fundamentally grounded in that sensory experience and shaped by it, if not empowered by it. While a thought sense is more questionable because it is further from experience, it does have merit. It may offer insight and even wisdom, but the way we can perceive that is to test it. We can feel if the thought sense resonates with our accumulated experience and our felt sense. This is something we will explore more when we discuss the viewing process.

Many meditative traditions have developed methodologies to counter the momentum of one thought sense generating another thought sense without ever connecting, reconnecting to, or resonating with, a felt sense. They generally accomplish this by encouraging us to develop a discipline that takes us back to the immediacy of our felt sense where we "see things as they are," which includes not only objects and our environment, but our thoughts, and even ourselves. Perceiving things as they are does not mean that we have given up on or are ignoring our thought sense in favor of felt sense alone.

Felt and Thought Senses Together

Any experience significantly lacking in either felt or thought sense would be incomplete and tenuous. Thoughts by

43

themselves, when they are not founded on experience, would seem to be empty thoughts and without substance as in a daydream. On the other hand, a felt sense that arises where there is no thought sense to capture it cannot be transformed into knowledge and ultimately wisdom. So it simply evaporates. Young children experience wonder all the time, but they have little or no thought sense to capture it and give it meaning. We also experience child-like wonder whenever we come upon something new and interesting. For many adults it seems that our wonder, which is connected to our felt sense, has been drummed out of us. When we encounter something new, we often feel compelled to meet it with skepticism and the need to identify and label it as fast as possible so we can move on to whatever is next, rather than explore it and enjoy our fascination.

As adults we could have the best of both: child-like wonder and the knowledge to enjoy it, which is felt sense and thought sense working together. Having both operating in concert offers a fuller life; when they are not working together we are disadvantaged. Malcolm Gladwell points out in his book *Blink*[6] that when the part of us that knows-without-thinking is operating without the benefit of the part that does think, unfortunate, if not tragic, situations can arise. He uses as an example the Getty's multimillion dollar purchase of a Kouros statue that is now considered to be a fake, as well as the tragic shooting death by police of an unarmed man, Amadou Diallo. With the purchase of the Kouros, everything appeared OK on paper: the documentation and scientific testing. However, experts familiar with how such statues look, "felt" at first glance there was something wrong with it. Although they could not prove it was a fake at the time, they felt it was and recommended that the Getty not purchase it. The felt sense of the statue lost out to the thought sense— the documentation. After the purchase, evidence surfaced to show where and how it was likely faked. Had the felt sense been allowed to inform the thought sense, maybe the purchase would not have been made. In the Diallo case, we have the opposite, where a few facts could have greatly informed a cascade of felt senses by several plain clothes officers and possibly prevented them from firing their weapons forty-one times, killing a frightened man. A man who stuttered while he attempted to take out his wallet for men he thought were robbing him in the hallway of his apartment building.

Felt and Thought Senses in Art

When thought and felt senses are in sync our experiences are clearer, truer, richer, and potentially sublime. Art and art-making are about experience, discovery, and sharing. Sharing involves communicating both the felt and thought sense of our inspiration through what we have created. As creative people, we make art by imbuing our inspiration with a form that will ideally recreate, or evoke, in the viewer the felt sense we originally experienced. Many works of art are created not only for others to feel something, but also to think something in response to their felt sense. This is because inspiration is often connected with some kind of realization. Depending on the style of artwork, the felt sense might be emphasized over thought sense or the reverse. For example, Expressionist art is tilted toward felt sense, and Conceptual art is tilted toward thought sense, but neither is absent the other. Regardless of their relative proportions to one another, felt and thought senses need to be present in artwork for it to have much effect on us. The greater their presence, the greater potential there is for experience and appreciation. Even when an artist claims that his or her work has no ideas, or thought sense, and nothing is being communicated, it is still communicating something. It is communicating the absence of something.

> *I sometimes feel that I have nothing to say and*
> *I want to communicate this.*

> ~Damien Hirst[7]

In everyday experience, felt and thought senses are at work regardless of how conscious we are of them. If we can become aware of them and how they work, we gain them as tools to help us with how we create and how we appreciate what we have created.

Chapter Six

Self-Expression and Pure Expression

Meditation practice brings into focus the nature of our experience, such as how felt and thought senses contribute to the fullness of our experience. At some point, practicing meditation brings to the surface the question of just who is experiencing the experiences. Who is the meditator doing the meditating? For art-makers and viewers, the question is, who is making and viewing the art? Such questions arise from time to time whether or not we meditate. However, having a meditation practice makes them ever-present; and engaging in a creative process makes them unavoidable. This is especially true if we see the fruition of our creative process as some form of self-expression.

What an art-maker brings to the creative process and the viewer brings to their perception of the final product is colored, if not overshadowed, by who we are. But who are we? Are we our egos, our sense of self? Ego is described as the experience of the self as separate from the world and others. Self is usually defined as our personality, distinguished from others. One of the most commonly stated purposes of making art is self-expression. From this point of view, originality is expressing our unique self in ways that others have not. Self-expression has been described as a vehicle of release or revealment akin to a catharsis or even exorcism. It can lead to self-discovery, self-styled psychotherapy, a source of income, prestige, pride, and historical immortality. It can also lead to intense self-consciousness, egotism, hesitation, creative blockages, and self-doubt.

Freedom from Self-Conscious Expression

When you do something, you should burn yourself completely,
like a good bonfire, leaving no trace of yourself.

~ Shunryu Suzuki Roshi[1]

There is another type of self-expression that is talked about in meditative traditions as well as by artists who found their self-consciousness and self-referencing in their expression claustrophobic and limiting and sought to transcend self in favor of a non-self-referencing form of expression. That style is pure expression.

Today, as you know, I am famous and very rich. But when I
am alone with myself, I haven't the courage to consider myself
an artist, in the great and ancient sense of that word.

~ Pablo Picasso[2]

A nonself-referencing, unselfconscious, or egoless approach to expression does not in any way mean the loss or absence of style and personality. It merely suggests that we do not have to be constantly referring back to whom we think we are while being creative or viewing. This approach does not see ego or the self as bad, neither does it argue that it should be denied nor eliminated. This approach merely sees the self-limiting nature of egoic expression. Especially when it leads to creative blockages.

Today, "multitasking" has entered our lexicon. We talk of multitasking, however, studies have recently shown that we really "multiswitch" rather than multitask. We switch between activities, sometimes slowly and sometimes quickly, producing the illusion of multitasking. Multiswitching means that when we switch our attention away from one activity to another, nothing is going on with the one we have switched away from. Therefore, if we are art-making and we switch to being self-conscious—thinking about ourselves as art-makers—our involvement in our creative process ceases until we once again switch back to art-making. This is made obvious in the use of traditional Asian papers in painting and calligraphy. Many traditional Asian papers are intentionally made with little or no sizing, in part to demonstrate the mindfulness of the artist. When you make a brushstroke with ink or watercolors on such paper, it must be done with confidence and without any hesitation. You must be fully present and one with the materials and your process. If you pause to self-reflect, or rethink what you are doing while doing it, the ink or paint will quickly bleed out and the form of brushstroke will be lost.

In the *Abhidharma*, an ancient Buddhist text on psychology, ego is described as a collection of subconscious tendencies driven by habitual actions in order to provide a sense of a continuous, solid self. It points out that as solid as our sense of self, or ego, might seem to us, it does not exist as an organ in our brain or body. Not only is ego seen as a habitual pattern, it creates and uses habits in a desire to efficiently perpetuate itself and the illusion of continuity.

Creativity involves the opposite. It means taking chances, going beyond habits, giving up security and our sense of continuity and the boundaries that separate us from our experience—all of which are very threatening to an ego that likes to be in complete control. Groundlessness, uncertainty, and uncomfortableness are not high-water marks for ego. Spontaneity suffers when ego is in constant control. Habitual actions are the opposite of sponta-neity. No wonder many artists have found their greatest struggle is with themselves.

Ego thinks it knows who we are, and it thinks *it* is who we are. In Buddhist psychology, ego, the sense of a separate self, is the seventh consciousness of eight that make up who we are.[3] The seventh consciousness is the one consciousness that can get too full of itself and end up distorting all the other conscious-nesses to serve itself.

> *The seventh is not only thinking "I," but it is thinking, "I am supreme. I am the best." It possesses the qualities of vanity and (being) imagined. It is vain in the sense of being futile and proud. It is imagined, because the basis of this experience is completely projected, the situation is completely imagined.*

~ Sakyong Mipham Rinpoche[4]

As mentioned previously, brain scans of experienced meditators show that the area of the brain concerned with orientation and awareness lights up when meditating, whereas the area concerned with self-referencing quiets down.[5] This appears to be a biological basis for the most important teach-ings found in the *Abhidharma*. If the self-imagined construct of ego were to relax and regain its balance with the other seven consciousnesses, who we truly are does not dissolve, it emerges. The egolessness frequently mentioned in meditative tradi-tions is not the absence of ego or the self, but the dissolution of the barrier between us and our world and our experience. Ego is about maintaining that separation, egolessness is about letting it go. Rather than being abstracted from our lives as if watching ourselves in some TV drama, we are living without imaginary boundaries. We are who we are and we do not need to constantly remind ourselves. When we see or feel something, we really see and feel it, rather than think and self-dialogue about seeing and feeling it.

Expressing Direct Experience is Pure Expression

From a nonego driven point of view, calling yourself an artist or not calling yourself an artist is unimportant either way. Creating a work of art, from this point of view, is the ordinary activity of being a complete human being, not the province of a special class of talented people we call "artists." Creating works of art is part of living everyday life to its fullest. It is a tool for staying in direct, unfiltered contact. Art created in this way tends to draw attention toward the work of art as opposed to its creator. There are cultures where artists do not sign their works, or if they do, they make up a name on the spot. A nonself-referencing form of expression "that transcends self and other," is called pure expression.

Self-expression, because of its self-referencing, is essentially about its maker and limited to that dimension. It is how its maker thinks of their world, thinks of their life, and thinks of their experience. Since by definition the self is separate from everything, they don't know if their thoughts are connected to anything other than themselves. Because of the "self" boundary they have created, everything could just be one gigantic self-dialogue.

When we produce work that is meaningful to ourselves, it may only be because we know our own visual or sensory language. It might have relevance to those who know us, share our views, or have had similar experiences. However, to anyone who does not know our artistic language, our work could be incomprehensible, demanding our intervention to explain it or translate it. Although commonly gallery exhibitions offer a written artist's statement in order to enrich the experience, it seems vital when the work does not stand on its own. There is certainly nothing at all wrong with limiting our audience to ourselves, our friends, or a specific group. It only becomes an issue if we are attempting to reach a larger audience—only to discover that we are not reaching them and do not know why.

Training to Go Beyond Self-Conscious Expression

The desire to step out of the way of ourselves is an intent that is so much easier to state than accomplish. We can find ourselves helping others without thought to ourselves, such as stopping a child before she races into a busy street. In our creative process, getting out of the way often involves trying to find a place to land, a state of mind in which our relentless self-referencing and self-dialoguing has quieted down. We, of course, can wait until it occurs by accident, or try some of the less effective means referred to earlier—or we can develop a meditation practice where one of the benefits is learning how to get out of our own way. Rather than keeping our attention on our thoughts about ourselves, meditation practice redirects us to the less egocentric task of following the breath. After gaining some stability in our meditation practice, we can transfer what we have learned, mindfulness, to our creative process where it becomes a meditation-in-action. We have an opportunity to practice becoming one with our process rather than one with our self-consciousness.

As said earlier, meditation synchronizes mind and body, and the right and left hemispheres of the brain. What this specifically means in terms of self-referencing and the absense of it is: The right side of the braining is connected with *perceiving* things as they are in terms of our felt sense, intuition, sense of nowness, and being a part of it all without self-referencing. Our left side is connected with *knowing* things as they are, the thought sense of things, keeping track of past and future, language, calculations, intellect, the "I am," and self-dialoguing. Sometimes our desire for efficiency leads us to be left-brain dependent. Meditation transforms our momentum for efficiency into one of appreciation. When we have both sides of the brain working together, our self-referencing and self-consciousness relax, and we find that our hesitation and doubt dissolve.

Because our felt and thought sense naturally order themselves in the practice of meditation and meditation-in-action, so does our intuition and intellect. In this way, our direct experience becomes the primary basis of our knowledge and understanding. When we are in sync, each side of ourselves informs the other and gathers a fuller picture of things as they are. When we are in sync, we are also expressing more fully who we are, as opposed to merely who we think we are. Self-centered expression naturally transforms into selfless expression, also known as pure expression.

Chapter Seven

Originality, Creativity, and Spontaneity

*Now and then, wandering through the streets, suddenly
one comes awake, perceives with a strange exultation that he
is moving through an absolutely fresh slice of reality ... It is as
if the eye itself had been freshened. The most commonplace
things are seen as if for the first time.*

~ Henry Miller[1]

When we practice meditation, sooner or later we have a moment of "nowness" when we are awake and aware, with no past or future, no beginning or end, and we are synchronized not only within ourselves, but with our environment. We may also realize that we experienced these moments before, but had not recognized them for what they were. When we are in such a moment, it is a departure from all others. It is unique. It is an original. Although we traveled a path to arrive at such a moment, such as the path of meditation, when it occurs it is not based on the past and it is not moving toward some future. The past and future are just a collection of thoughts that have evaporated like a fog meeting the heat of the sun. We have discovered something that is self-existing and yet unborn. If there is anything that could ever be considered truly original, it would be this moment, this space: original space.

Whatever directly arises in this space is truest and most accurate to that experience. It is not distorted, at least not yet. It arises within our consciousness and becomes knowable as our felt sense, our intuitive intelligence, and it may be trusted. If at that moment some self-referencing thought stream takes shape and we follow it, it will likely lead us away from original space and originality.

When the experience of original space occurs, at first we may be timid when such intuitive intelligence arises out of it. If we act on that intelligence, we find that more often than not it "works" for us and that accomplishment encourages us to go further. Original space is the place, the landing zone, we are working—consciously or not—to arrive at. It is a place where something original can surface.

This original space, this synchronicity, as powerful and magical as it is, is only the first step in the creative process. As with many first steps, they are fragile and can readily be diverted. In truth, what is more likely to happen in the beginning is the frustration of finding the moment is lost and our original inspiration mired in a self-conscious thought stream. This happens because our self-referencing returns and reasserts itself in order to own the moment and claim the inspiration. It takes additional meditation practice to relax this tendency, and we will eventually find that coming back to original space is as natural as coming back to the breath in meditation practice.

Our contact with original space can occur accidentally, spontaneously, or with some regularity through the discipline we develop in meditation. As we practice, we find that even if we lose contact with original space, it will eventually return.

We don't have to squeeze the moment dry in order to get something out of it. We can let ourselves be present in the nowness, which encourages more of these moments.

> *It is not necessary that you leave the house. Remain at*
> *your table and listen. Do not even listen, only wait.*
> *Do not even wait, be wholly still and alone. The world will*
> *present itself to you for its unmasking, it can do no other,*
> *in ecstasy it will writhe at your feet.*

~ Franz Kafka[2]

Turning Autopilot Off

We have learned there is a great deal that prevents us from arriving at original space, and when we do arrive, our conditioning frequently obscures it. Conditioned activities, or habitual patterns, are the antithesis of being fully present and spontaneous. Why did we develop habits in the first place? Because it takes less effort to follow a habit than to pay attention to the details of our life. Paying attention can be exhausting. So we create patterns or conditioned responses as a kind of autopilot in order to mentally free ourselves from what we feel are the mundane tasks of life. During the times when we are not on autopilot, whatever is happening in the present moment is often regarded as unsatisfying or boring. And if it is satisfying and desirable, we worry about how long it will last or how good or bad it will be. By then we are out of the present moment and back in autopilot mode.

In contrast, direct experience requires turning off autopilot and being mindful in each and every moment. We have to pay attention to the details in *and* around us, whether they are exciting and interesting or dull and boring. However, we cannot accomplish this by simply becoming hypervigilant. That truly *is* exhausting. In order to accomplish mindfulness, we have to slow down our discursive mind and relax our self-centeredness. This frees us up to, in a relaxed way, pay greater attention to the whole moment because *we* are no longer the primary focus of our attention.

From the point of view of mindfulness, paying attention to something is simply resting our senses on whatever presents itself. But because the activity of mindfulness is an inclusive process, in order to do it we have to let go of our selectivity, editing, and editorializing about what we pay attention to. If we ignore one thing in favor of another, we are not being mindful. Mindfulness means paying attention not only when it is pleasurable to do so but also when it is not. *Any* editing or embellishing not only takes us away from mindfulness and being in the moment but also leads us back into our old habits and conditioning. When we dull ourselves to one thing, we cannot but help dull ourselves a little bit to everything else.

Sometimes it takes a personal crisis that is too great for our habitual patterns, our autopilot, to smooth over. Crisis forces us to wake up to mindfulness. Maybe it takes a health issue, an economic necessity, or needs of others that we can no longer ignore to discover that our mind and body have been living two separate lives. Our body has been present, but our mind has been elsewhere. I have heard it described that our mind and body can be like a tired old married couple who live in the same house but only communicate with each other when there is a crisis.

Life is what happens while you are making other plans.

~ John Lennon[3]

Over the course of our lifetime, we can become so practiced at being out of direct touch that it feels like we need the mental equivalent of a machete to hack our way through the dense jungle of our conditioning to get to original space. At the same time, if we put too much energy behind our blade in the form of anger, frustration, and ego, we end up planting seeds for new growth in our jungle as we destroy the old. The notion of reaping what we sow, or the principle of karma—cause and effect—refers not only to the "bad" things we do, but also how we accomplish the "good" things.

Emptying the Idea of Art

We try not to have ideas, preferring accidents. To create, you must empty yourself of every artistic thought.

~ Gilbert (of Gilbert and George)[4]

As Gilbert points out, our artistic thoughts can also develop into their own kind of autopilot, preventing us from being in the moment and manifesting spontaneity. Concentration can also work against us. By concentration, I mean not only focusing on our goal but ignoring everything else in the process. It takes a great deal of work to suppress what we are trying to forget or ignore. It could be past artistic successes or failures, or simply what distracts us in our environment while engaging in our creative process. When concentrating, a part of our mind has to actively monitor and stand ready to pounce on anything that might enter our consciousness other than our goal. All this divides our energy and leaves little for being in original space. If we hope to arrive at and be in original space, we need to practice letting go of agendas, conditioning, concentration, and emotional conflicts and come back to our senses to perceive with "fresh eyes."

There is nothing more difficult for a truly creative painter
than to paint a rose, because before he can do so he has first
to forget all the roses that were ever painted.

~ Henri Matisse[5]

Just as meditation practice involves letting go and perceiving each moment with fresh eyes, Matisse's quote points out that the creative process involves the same. A meditation practice is a perfect way to learn how to let go, and that we *can* let go. We also learn that it is beneficial to let go of not only distractions and thoughts that take us away from original space, but also things that we desire—like artistic ideas. It might seem like heresy for an artist to let go of an artistic inspiration, however, the payoff for not grasping what arises during our meditation practice is that we create a stable environment for inspiration to arise more frequently within our meditation, our creative process, and life as a whole. At some point, our practice is mature enough that when an inspiration arises and we have let it go, it frequently reappears naturally in post-meditation. This encourages us to relax further and trust our meditation practice as a path to developing our creative process as a form of meditation-in-action. A formal meditation practice leads toward creating a mental environment where original space arises all the time, not only in our creative process, but everywhere, even in our sleep. It becomes part of our being.

Spontaneity in Expression

There is more to spontaneity than caprice or disorder.

~ Alan Watts[6]

One of the desirable by-products of being in original space is spontaneity. True spontaneity surfaces in an environment of discipline. Ordinarily we see discipline and spontaneity as mutually exclusive, but the discipline we are concerned with here is the practice of coming back to nowness and original space. In meditation we do this by placing our attention on the breath. During post-meditation, as our attention shifts to our senses or our creative process as meditation-in-action, it is discipline that keeps us in touch with the present moment and all that is happening. We cannot be spontaneous if we are out of touch. The word "spontaneous" comes from the Latin spontāneus, which means "of one's own accord." Spontaneity is an activity that comes from a natural inclination. It's not planned or provoked by external incitement. It is not impulsiveness. Impulsiveness is spontaneity with an overlay of aggression and speed—more a reaction than a response. And spontaneity does not happen automatically, which implies something without thought or conscious engagement.

When we are truly spontaneous, we are wakeful, present, and tuned in. Our senses are alive. Spontaneity does not have the self-conscious reactiveness of impulsiveness because there is no separation between us and the environment. When we are tuned into the environment, we have synchronized our mind and body with it. In such a moment the spontaneous activity that occurs is an expression of that synchronicity, and therefore it is also accurate. It conforms to the moment with precision and accuracy.

True spontaneity is linked to accuracy but for them to work in concert within the creative process, spontaneity must come first—just as our felt sense should precede thought sense. If instead accuracy comes first, we separate ourselves from our environment in an attempt to objectify, study, compare, and measure its contents to record them. Spontaneity is lost: we are no longer one with our environment but instead have become a detached observer of it. To be truly spontaneous within our creative process, and for that matter everyday life, we need to be one with our environment. It is that oneness, the lack of separation and self-consciousness and second guessing that often follows, which allows us to be more accurate.

By definition, we cannot plan a spontaneous moment. We can either wait for it to occur by accident or we can engage a discipline to invite it. There is no better invitation to spontaneity than being in original space. The energy for spontaneity does not need to be manufactured because when we are not tied up with our self-referencing it is ever present and manifests out of our innate inquisitiveness: our human passion to look, to play, to know, to understand, and then to communicate.

Figure 5 : *"Kongo" or "Vajra" in Sanskrit, "Diamond-like" in English,*
by Taizen Maezumi Roshi

Chapter Eight

Signs and Symbols

Art does not reproduce the visible;
rather, it makes visible.

~ Paul Klee[1]

Even when our mind, body, and environment are synchronized and our self-referencing is quiet for a few moments, we cannot say that we are free of bias. Bias here refers to a preferential point of view, a loyalty to our specific perception and the style in which we perceive it. Most often, bias has a negative connotation because it indicates an incomplete or limited view, a self-styled view. But if self-referencing is absent in our minds, bias is just the manifestation of our objective subjectivity, in which we have some objectivity regarding our subjectivity. In other words, we notice that we have a point of view, but also know that it is not the only view. For example, two people are looking at a sculpture from two different angles. Let us say one person is young and one is old. Each point of view would likely be influenced by their accumulated years of experience as well as their relative physical position to the sculpture. We could add other differences: education, experience, and so on. But regardless of the differences, one point of view does not contradict the other—instead it can inform the other. They are parts of a larger whole. The more points of view we gather, the closer we get to a complete picture.

An ego-driven bias, on the other hand, does not try to gather more points of view, but instead asserts the superiority of its own point of view over all others. It assumes it has captured the whole picture and is more insightful than others. An ego-driven point of view is tied up with a sense of identity, and differing viewpoints are seen as personal challenges.

If we could be truly unbiased, egoless, and achieve multiple, simultaneous points of view based on full knowledge of what we encounter, we *would* have a superior view because we would be enlightened! A more practical achievement would be to become aware of our specific biases and then work to include other viewpoints to transcend the limitations of our bias. We almost always see things, or feel what is communicated, or express things in different ways, in different times and circumstances. In other words, we are unique; each moment is unique; and that's not a problem as long as we are not constantly self-reflecting on our uniqueness and asserting it as superior to others. As long as we can drop our self-referencing, our bias is about appreciating circumstances rather than manifesting egotism. And because we can see our bias, we may be able to see through it to glimpse things as they are and more fully perceive what they are communicating.

What Is Being Communicated?

Let's say we are looking at a rock we just found and we perceive it as it is from a specific angle, time of day, through our eyeglasses, and so on. In other words, we perceive it through our bias.

We could ask ourselves, "Is the rock communicating anything other than its rockness?" To even begin to answer that, we first have to ask ourselves, "What is the nature of communication itself, on the simplest level, such as when I am simply viewing?" When something is being communicated, what is it and how does it do it? Does communication require a sender or can things communicate themselves without one? Let's explore what is being communicated when we perceive things as they are.

On a fundamental level, we perceive both surface and substance. Surface perception is basically any information that is being communicated. For example, we look at rock and we perceive its colors, its size, its weight, and we recognize it as a rock and maybe we even know what kind of rock it is. It is mainly the perception of the thought sense of things. Substance perception is based more on the felt presence that is being communicated, its felt sense, its "rockness." Substance perception is what we experience about the object regardless of what we know about it.

Meditation Exercise on Surface and Substance

The meditation that follows is designed to make this point clear by highlighting the difference between these two perceptions. *If you skip this meditation and just read on, it will only reinforce the mistaken belief that the thought sense of things is enough.*

Here is the instruction. Begin by finding an object that is the size of a golf ball so it will fit in your hand. The more personal the object is to you, the better. Get something to write with.

Take the posture you use to practice meditation. Place the object in front of you so you can comfortably see it while in your meditation posture. Ideally, there should be some space around it with no other objects in direct view. Take a few moments to write anything you want about the object.

Next, you are going to meditate with your eyes open and resting on your personal object. In this meditation, you return to the object rather than your breath every time you drift off. Do this for a minimum of twenty-five minutes. If you compromise on the time by shortening it, you will significantly reduce the possibility of experiencing what we will discuss later.

After twenty-five to thirty minutes, retrieve your writing materials and take a few moments to write about the object, as well as your experience.

Now, please stop reading this instruction and go ahead with the exercise. Once you have completed the meditation, read on.

Read what you wrote before and after the meditation to yourself, preferably out loud. Do you notice a difference? If so, what? Here is what many people discover.

At first, before we meditate on the object, most of us write about our personal connection to the object and what it represents to us. For example, we might recall how we acquired it, or who gave it to us, and all the feelings and circumstances associated with it flood into our mind. This can send us off on a long journey of memories.

After meditating on the object, the writing is usually a mix of personal history and details and characteristics possessed by the object that we had not previously noticed. And, significantly, we saw something about the object that is independent of its history. Let us say the object is a rock crystal that a beloved parent collected and handed down to us as a keepsake. The object evokes all kinds of memories and feelings. However, after sitting with it for an extended period of time, there is usually at least one moment in which the personal history evaporates and the rock crystal is seen simply as a rock crystal. It is seen as anyone else might see it without knowing the object's history.

You might have found yourself a little bored with your object, but if you stayed with it, its qualities and characteristics likely took center stage. You might have noticed its roughness, smoothness, transparency, reflectiveness, and color. You may have begun to appreciate what it is, simply, without any attachments to it.

The purpose of this exercise is not to learn to devalue our personal attachment to things that we treasure, but to experience the fact that objects communicate to us in two ways. They communicate their physical presence as well as reflect back the information we know or discover about them: their felt sense as well as their thought sense. If we can see that communication has two types, the felt and thought sense of things, we have just acquired a powerful tool in art-making and art-viewing. When we are not aware of these two aspects, or forget one of them, we are missing half of what is being communicated. For instance, in order to create a sculpture, collage, or installation, we might use a number of objects that have great personal interest, meaning, and history for us. If people come to see it and do not have the same personal interest and cannot read our minds, they perceive what appears to be a collection of stuff and little beyond that is communicated. If what we are attempting to share is not inherently present in the objects, then we might wish to consider how we could communicate that additional experience or knowledge. But we cannot begin to do that unless we can at least glimpse what we create as others might see it.

Only a Rose is a Rose

Symbols and signs are the two vehicles for communication in the arts. They are respectively the felt sense and thought sense of what is being communicated. They are what we directly experience and what we know about what is being presented. To appreciate these two vehicles, let's explore the word "rose" and a rose. The word "rose," is certainly not a rose. It's merely a word that refers to a rose. If the letters of the word **rose** were colored red, it would not change the word into an actual rose. It might, however, be a word that now indicates a red rose, but it is not itself a red rose.

What about a drawing or an illustration of a rose? Is this a rose?

Figure 6: *Illustration of a Rose*

No, it is a picture of a rose. Like the word "rose" it serves the same purpose in that it refers to a rose. Whether we have the word "rose," a graphic of a rose, an illustration of a rose, a photo of a rose, or even a silk rose, none of them are roses. At the same time, there is a difference between each of them in that one may more fully point our mind toward what a rose is than another; however, none is any more a rose than the other. Only a rose is a rose. It could be argued that the words and pictures are types of roses. They may be types of representations of a rose, but none of them can truly be taken for a real rose of any kind. A rose is a rose, is a rose and would be a rose by any other name. The name, the surface characteristics, and all we know about roses are not the substance of the rose. They alone do not determine the complete nature of the object. An actual rose, in addition to its surface characteristics, has a felt presence, felt experience, or felt sense that is not matched by any words, allusions, or descriptions.

Perceiving with Fresh Eyes

The example of the rose points out that we have two types of communication, our direct experience of a rose, its substance, and what we know or think about it.

> *If you have a glass full of liquid you can discourse forever on*
> *its qualities, discuss whether it is cold, warm, whether it is*
> *really and truly composed of H2O, or mineral water, or saki.*
> *Zazen[2] [meditation practice] is drinking it.*

~ Taisen Deshimaru[3]

Deshimaru encourages us to not confuse our knowledge of something for the experience of it. When we are presented with any unfamiliar object, as opposed to an object with personal history, we naturally explore it and play with it: touching it, turning it, seeing if it rattles, if it smells, maybe even taste it as would a child. We are naturally inquisitive. We gather all the sensory information we can. If we are scientists and have a laboratory we might even perform experiments on it. If we cannot figure out what it is, we might go to the extent of asking someone if they know. When we finally find out what it is, our immediate reaction is generally of surprise and we experience an "ah-ha" moment. At that instant, something shifts, the object seems changed by the knowledge, our labeling, and recognition. When you look at it again, it is no longer with the same intense child-like interest. It becomes merely another object to be mentally inventoried with countless others. We have had our experience with it—now it is time to move on to whatever is next. With our interest satisfied, we have little need to revisit it or labor to reexperience it. The freshness seems gone. But the freshness is not really gone in the object. The object is unchanged. It is gone in ourselves. But is it permanently lost?

> *Very few people look,*
> *most just try to identify what they see.*

> ~ Henri Cartier-Bresson[4]

This process of labeling and pigeonholing can be a problem for the creative and viewing processes. The ability to reexperience familiar objects and events with fresh eyes, ears, nose, and so on, is vital to the creative process as well as viewing the final result we call "art." If we cannot revisit what we perceive with freshness, we end up working with only our personal history and lexicon rather than directly with the objects, materials, or processes themselves. Without the ability to have a fresh experience with familiar objects and environments, we become increasingly insular. We generate knowledge based on our imagination rather than knowledge based on direct experience. This usually leads us back to what we already think we know. Artwork created in this way, as we have said, appears to be more of a self-conversation than communication with others. This is not at all an argument against using events in one's life as the means to communicate or make art. Using one's personal history has been one of the greatest resources mined by many of the world's treasured artists. A writer's specific historical events can be used in a way that transcends the author's personal boundary to communicate some common humanity, view, realization, or truth. In order to transcend our personal boundaries we need to see our work as others might—without the context we imbue it with. We need to be able to see it with fresh eyes.

Communication depends on a common basis. On the surface, it can be a common language. However, on the level of substance, or felt sense, it takes place through shared, unfiltered, direct experience of what is perceived. In order for this to occur, both creator and viewer must be able to reexperience familiar objects and environments in the same manner as unfamiliar ones, with unconditioned perception. Allowing perception to precede recognition and labeling is the means to experiencing and reexperiencing the world with freshness. This is accomplished by extending the discipline, mentioned earlier, of arriving at original space and broadening our awareness to include the perceived objects or events. It is possible to let go of everything we know for at least a brief moment to reexperience things unconditionally, as we do in meditation.

In order to explain the nature of perception in more detail, meditative traditions have described two aspects: our sense perceptions and our sense consciousnesses (the consciousness of a sense perception). This is helpful in understanding the fact that not all that our eyes, ears, etc., perceive rises to the level of consciousness. Cognitive science estimates that some eleven million bits of information are sensed every second, but only a tiny fraction—some one to two hundred bits per second—rise to the level of consciousness.[5] Whether through laziness or simple exhaustion, rather than trying to expand the number of bits that rise to the level of consciousness, our brain or mind opts for conjecture and preconceptions to fill in what it has discarded or missed.

This differentiation of sense perceptions and sense consciousnesses can help us to also see how our thoughts may affect the consciousness of our perceptions. A familiar example is the story of someone who is terrified of snakes suddenly coming upon a coiled rope and mistaking it for a snake. In such an instance, the eyes perceive something, the eye consciousness reports it to the mind, but if the mind is fearful of snakes and snake-like images, it may pounce on that perception and alter it so the mind registers "snake" rather than "rope."

When our sense perceptions and their subsequent sense consciousnesses are left undisturbed by our hopes and fears, they naturally progress from perception to consciousness to a felt sense and then to our thought sense. When we interfere with this order by allowing hopes and fears (which are thought senses) to insert themselves in the form of a projection (also a thought sense), our conscious mind registers the projection rather than the reality: a snake, rather than the rope. After all, the aforementioned study shows our mind is primed for conjecture and preconception to begin with. But a little fear goes a long way, so when a projection occurs, we are ready to react to it as if it is the real thing.

Meditation helps us to depart from such a path through the development of peacefulness and what is called "calm abiding." Meditation, over time, does reduce the amount of fear we experience. This reduces the number of fear-induced projections and with fewer projections to react to, we have less to fear, which in turn leads to bravery. Meditation will not provide abilities we do not have, but it can provide us a path to utilizing more fully what we do have, such as the ability to see things more as they truly are. One can, even if for only brief moments, stop filtering and editing, and see through one's thoughts, biases, and conditioning to what is.

If we manage to perceive with fresh senses, and a fresh mind, then our creative process becomes direct and very powerful and the result is more likely to communicate the same. This is because we are working with the fundamental nature of things as they are. It can almost seem magical to work with things in this way. In this case, magic is about evoking a sense of wonderment and openness in the viewer. Some argue that magic is about fooling people, tricking them, but magic can be seen as playing with our senses—what we do and do not perceive—in order to evoke a particular experience: wonderment. This happens not only in a successful magic act but also when we see something we have never seen before in a work of art and are inexplicably taken by it.

Distinguishing Knowledge from Experience

There are examples in which the boundary between our thoughts about things and the things themselves are particularly difficult to perceive, especially when we spend so much time thinking about things rather than experiencing them. Another mental experiment might illustrate this point. If we imagine someone spoke the word "table" and for whatever reason we did not know what the word meant, we might look it up in a dictionary. There we would find a definition of the word "table," maybe even a picture of a table, but not an actual table—same as with the example of the rose. The dictionary only possesses words that refer to other words, that refer to yet other words, in an endless cycle. The dictionary is absent of any objects it defines, except itself as a "dictionary." For everything else, a dictionary is free of the substance of all that it defines.

If we take the opposite approach and observe an actual table and were asked to describe it, we would likely begin by calling it a table. If asked to, we might go into greater specificity and describe the table. Depending on our background, we might add descriptions of its composition, its chemistry, engineering, history and so on. If we were to write all of that information down and looked at it all, would it amount to being a table? No, it would be an elaborate description, but it would be no more a table than the words found in a dictionary. We cannot fashion an actual table with writings about it. Knowledge of a table does not constitute a table and a table does not need to be recognized and labeled to place a vase on it. The table exists independently of our knowledge.

If we could imagine for a moment removing all our knowledge regarding the table, the table does not disappear along with the information. There is the table *and* there is our knowledge regarding the table: two very distinct perceptions. We cannot in actuality remove our knowledge from a known object because the two are as inseparable as the waves are from the ocean. Yet we can know there is a difference between the ocean and its waves. In the same way, we can distinguish between our knowledge and our experience. Because we can perceive this difference, it is possible to be able to *see through* our knowledge to the thing itself and reexperience it unconditionally. If this were not true, we could not see the difference between our thoughts and our experience. Because we can, it is possible to also see the true nature of signs and symbols.

A Deeper Understanding of Symbol

Signs and symbols are the language of art. Their relationship to one another is difficult to unravel unless we include the notions of thought and felt senses found in meditative traditions. A reason why signs and symbols can be so difficult to understand in our culture is due to the limitations of the English language. One could argue that English is a relatively new language and in its development has left behind some of the more experiential meanings found in older languages. In any case, we become acutely aware of its limitations with the definition of the word, "symbol." If we looked "sign" and "symbol" up in a dictionary, we would find that their definitions do not sound all that different from one another and seem almost interchangeable.

But they are different. A sign is generally defined as words or images that point toward something, like a stop sign, a road sign, or a sign that says, "Handicap Parking Only." All these signs are about communicating information. A sign is simply a vehicle similar to the way the word "table" is the vehicle that conveys the idea of a table.

A symbol seems to be defined as an abstract kind of sign, such as a $ sign. For example, we are driving and we see a display by a check-cashing service with the word "money." That would be a sign for money. If that word were replaced with $$$, that would be an example of a symbol for money, and probably a lot of money. In English, sign and symbol convey the same information, but in slightly different packaging.

Another example would be that we could have a sign that says with words "No Smoking" or we could convey the same message with the pictograph for no smoking.

Figure 7: *No Smoking Symbol*

Such pictographs are commonly called "symbols" and are frequently used as substitutes for posting language-dependent messages. They become a type of international language for cultures who have agreed about their meaning. Words and pictographs both convey information.

Often, English dictionaries use the difference in appearance as sufficient reason to classify pictographs as symbols. Some dictionaries go a bit further and describe a symbol as a type of sign that refers to a deeper, hidden meaning or message, where some secret information is being communicated to those who share the key to its meaning. Another source attempts to distinguish a "natural symbol"[6] from other symbols in that it does not require any agreement. It is understood universally and naturally like the sun as the symbol of life and strength and a river as the symbol of eternal change.

All these definitions essentially characterize a symbol as a subcategory of sign rather than on par with it. Symbols are, in one form or another, vehicles that transmit information as do signs. But in art and other endeavors, we have many examples of symbols being used to convey much more than information.

Symbol as Embodied Experience

The map is not the territory.

~ Alfred Korzbyski[7]

This quote, as did Deshimaru's, warns us not to confuse information about something for its reality, its experience. It points us to look beyond the signage. But what is beyond the signage? It would also seem that Rene Magritte's 1929 painting *The Treachery of Images*, communicates a similar idea with the words "Ceci n'est pas une pipe" (This is not a pipe) painted underneath a realist painting of a smoker's pipe. A painted pipe, or the word "pipe," is not a pipe. From this point of view any word, picture, graphic, or sign of any kind should not be confused for the experience of the thing itself. If the reality of the thing itself is not its information or its signage, then what word do we use to call it?

Symbol, in this sense, is not a "sign" representing some philosophical or religious principle; it is the demonstration of the living qualities of what is.

~ Chögyam Trungpa Rinpoche[8]

The view expressed in this quote goes back to the third-century Indian Madhyamakan[9] meditative and philosophical view in which a symbol is the direct experience of the thing itself. We experience its symbolism when we approach it with a meditative state of mind. This tradition predates the English definition of symbol. From this third-century point of view, a symbol is not a sign of any kind. A symbol is not about conveying information; instead it is embodying an experience. For example, a Zen teacher holds up a tree branch and asks a student, "What is this?" The student says, "It is a branch from a tree." The teacher says, "No, it is not." The teacher asks the now-confused student again and again what it is, and when the resigned student responds with, "Well, if it is not a branch, then what is it?" The master suddenly strikes him with the branch. The Master then says, "That's what it is," and the student understands that the tree branch is not its label, its description, or any information about it, but instead the experience of it.

Whatever makes a pipe a pipe, or a branch a branch, it does not depend on anything other than itself. An actual pipe or branch is not a sign for anything; rather, they totally embody and communicate themselves without the need for language. From this point of view, symbols are things that directly communicate themselves. They do not point to anything else.

Direct communication was also the goal of the Non-objective Abstract Art movement, which began in the early 1910s. Symbols, and such artwork, communicate their fullness: the complete reality of itself. The nonconceptual direct experience of something is sometimes translated as "isness" or "suchness." Isness is the full experience without labels, thoughts, and emotions superimposed. The word "nature" in Chinese is sometimes translated as "that which is so of itself." Unless we superimpose some message on it, the living rose is not a sign pointing toward something else. It embodies "roseness" and is therefore a symbol of itself just as pipe is a symbol of itself, and painting a symbol of itself, and so on.

This notion of isness, direct experience, is difficult to convey in words because to realize it one must ultimately surrender words and labels in favor of the experience. Symbols are grasped by experiencing them directly.

People's usual idea of symbolism is that it is something outside them, like a signpost or billboard, that gives them signs, perhaps of religious significance. That's not quite true ... Symbolism is based on what we experience personally and directly in our lives: pain, pleasure, or whatever. From that point of view, symbolism is a state of mind.

~ Chögyam Trungpa Rinpoche[10]

From this point of view, a symbol is on equal footing and in contrast to a sign. Not only can a symbol be clearly distinguished from a sign, it serves to define it. Sign and symbol define the other. A symbol represents what cannot be represented in any other way: itself, its isness. A sign is the opposite and is not about itself. It is about conveying information about something other than itself. Sign and symbol are knit. Symbols are nonconceptual forms of direct communication that appeal to an intuitive felt sense. They are nonconceptual messages without a messenger in that they communicate their isness. Signs are messengers in that they communicate information. Just as the word "table" is not a three-dimensional table, signage has no substance of its own. Signs point toward other signs and information, *and* they can point toward symbols and their inherent substance.

A wonderful demonstration of the differences between the physical presence of an object, a picture of it, and its dictionary definition, is an art piece by Joseph Kosuth, entitled, *Une et trois chaises (One and Three Chairs)*. It places a chair between a photo of the same chair and a placard with the definition of the word "chair".[11] This work calls into question what makes a chair a chair. In this example, is a chair its label, its definition, a picture of it, or its physical presence? What is its signage and what is its symbolism? Since the three aspects are also presented as an art piece, it also raises the issue of when a chair is merely a chair and when and if it can also be a work of art.

If we were inspired by Kosuth's predecessor Marcel Duchamp and his Ready-mades[12] and placed a single chair in a gallery and labeled it as a sculpture that was entitled, *Chair*, does it now become a work of art or is it still the same chair it has always been? Have we changed anything by virtue of its new label and location? If one calls a chair a "sculpture," does that mean you can no longer sit in it? If you can sit in a sculpture, does it become a chair because it serves that function? Our notions of what makes a chair a chair and a sculpture a sculpture are being challenged. Duchamp and Kosuth's art work are like western Zen koans. A koan is an apparently contradictory or impossible riddle that is given to a student by a Zen meditation master. It cannot be solved through rational thought processes alone, but due to human inquisitiveness one cannot stop trying. After innumerable attempts at a logical solution, the thinking mind exhausts itself and gives up; stops for a brief moment without labels, without thought patterns. There is just original space, your awareness, and the koan, and then suddenly it is understood.

In the case of the chair-sculpture koan, we might get the direct experience, the symbolism of chairness and sculptureness as opposed to their signage or labels.

> *But once we stop rejecting the world, the world begins to pounce on us. Symbolism is imposed on us. Realizations and perceptions of all kinds of realities begin to take shape. There is symbolism right and left and front and back.*
>
> ~ Chögyam Trungpa Rinpoche[13]

Symbolism is presenting itself all the time and it is readily available to us if we only penetrate the surface knowledge of things to the substance below. If we perceive only surface, then artwork communicates only surface information. If we also perceive substance, then artwork can additionally communicate itself with a sense of presence and evoke a powerful direct experience within us. A work of art becomes a symbol of itself when it attempts to communicate what cannot be communicated in any other way. The more effectively it communicates its presence, the more it transcends signage and becomes a symbol.

Art education makes itself vital when it puts knowledge into proper perspective through teaching the value of direct experience. The living quality of knowledge is found in presence, substance, symbol, and direct experience.

Symbol in Art Making

When we work on the level of substance and symbolic qualities, we are working with the fundamental nature of things and our work reflects that. What we make moves out of the realm of being merely curious, entertaining, thoughtful, or interesting, to being evocative and transforming. When we perceive the symbolism around us, we are directly communicating with our world. There is no need to anthropomorphize the messages and assume someone or something is sending it. We can simply perceive the world's messages: messages without a messenger. In this context, a message is communicating something, but that something is purely "isness." If there is meaning to be had from the message, it usually comes in a flash of insight, or first thought, that occurs naturally and immediately after our experience of its isness.

First thought is best in art, second in other matters.

~ William Blake[14]

We can either take that "first thought" as it is and work with it as it is, or we can twist it into something that is disconnected from what it is. In microseconds we can turn that first thought into a discursive thought and then into many thoughts and lose any immediacy that the first thought held for us. We can then reintroduce self-referencing by asking such questions as "Why is this happening to me?" and "What's the meaning of it all?" which separates us further from our original experience and any symbolism, any direct realization. Alternatively, by staying with the isness of the moment we glimpse the messages. They communicate through us as our first thoughts and insights, and manifest as originality.

Signs and symbols are interdependent and present in all things perceived; however, they are in differing proportions. It is like the earlier analogy with the waves and the ocean, in which we can perceive two distinct things: the waves and the ocean. At the same time, each is inseparable from the other. There are times when the ocean is so still, there are barely any waves and all we can see is a vast ocean. At other times, the waves of a storm can be so huge that an oncoming wave seems like the entire ocean unto itself. When we explored the word "rose" in comparison to the actual living rose, we had examples that were in between the two, from the word "**rose**" in red letters, to an illustration of the rose, a photograph of the rose, and a silk rose. None of which are an actual rose. Nevertheless, each is slightly more rose-like. We can see there is a shift, an almost sliding scale in which each has successively captured a bit more of the characteristics that give the rose its presence, its symbolism. Each example has its own felt presence, some of which is more rose-like than others.

Signs and symbols work the same way in all forms of art. Art is a symbol of itself because it is the thing itself and it communicates itself. In addition, the art might contain within itself signs and symbols. Artwork that uses primarily signage and imagery that refers to other artworks or information tend to point the viewer *away* from the artwork and toward what is referenced.

Parodies and homages to other artwork are abundant in art and to understand them you must be knowledgeable about what is being referenced. With this type of artwork signage has a prominent role.

There is also artwork that does not seem to depend on any references and stands on its own. I mentioned Non-objective Abstract Art. Purely viewing it directly is often sufficient to experience and appreciate what it is about. One art form is not better than another. What determines value in this discussion is whether what is communicated is clearly communicated and if it is connected with the intent, or inspiration, of the artist.

In the creative process, understanding the nature of sign and symbol turns each into an instrument for expression and communication. Depending on how we use them, we can direct viewers away from our work to some other experience or present our work as the experience itself. However, to accomplish either, we need to be able to perceive things as they are. We need to be able to feel the redness of red, the stoniness of stone, the isness quality of things in order to have any chance of communicating substance as well as surface.

Chapter Nine

The Creative Process as Meditation-in-Action

*A haiku is not a poem, it is not literature; it is a
hand becoming, a door half-opened, a mirror wiped clean.
It is a way of returning to nature, to our moon nature,
our cherry blossom nature, our falling leaf nature,
in short, to our Buddha nature.*

~ Reginald H. Blyth[1]

As we develop a formal meditation practice, the mindfulness and awareness we experience naturally seeps into everyday life activities. As art-makers this would include our creative process. As our meditation practice strengthens, we find ourselves applying the same discipline to our creative process. During formal practice the object of meditation is our breath and now our creative process becomes the object of our mindfulness and awareness practice. In this way, the creative process develops into a form of meditation-in-action. Meditation-in-action can be applied to any task, but our main concern here is how it benefits the creative process and, as we will see later, how it clarifies the viewing process.

The creative process as a meditation-in-action practice encompasses coming to original space, being in original space, and returning to it when we drift off from it, as well as being aware of the nature of what arises in that space and how to work with it. If what arises is the kind of self-consciousness and self-dialoguing that threatens to steal us away from pure expression, we can exercise our discipline of letting it go and returning to original space, which is simply where we are.

When we do arrive at where we are, our meditation-in-action practice can go awry when we find ourselves waiting in ambush for some inspiration to arise. It is useful to adopt the view that we are explorers ready for discovery rather than predators waiting for prey. During formal meditation practice, we can often feel that shift to being a predator because we tighten and tense up. Since our creative process is a more active process, it can be challenging to be aware of such a shift. However, when we do become aware of it, we relax and return to where we are. In truth, our awareness of it helps us to relax.

Meditation-in-action is not meant to be a substitute for formal meditation. Without a formal practice, it is too easy for us to get caught up in an activity and think we are doing meditation-in-action when we are really just self-absorbed. Here again, this can be a challenge to know the difference. Mindfulness practice can lead us to a greater degree of awareness, or its opposite, self-absorption. Because of this, awareness is vital to the creative process. Self-absorption is a hindrance because it abstracts us from our environment and cuts us off from our senses and the world. If our art-making has anything to do with communicating direct experience and things as they are to others, it would seem self-absorption is unhelpful. However, when we are in some kind of creative flow and totally immersed, how can we know if we are self-absorbed or not? We can usually tell by whether we have kept or lost our awareness of our environment. Meditation-in-action is an inclusive practice in which the mindfulness we develop leads us to a greater awareness, not to greater concentration. We are learning to open up, not narrow down.

Because it is difficult to hide from ourselves in formal mind-fulness *and* awareness meditation practice, we can be honest with ourselves and avoid self-deceptions and self-absorption. Engaging in both meditation and meditation-in-action practices supports the integration of mindfulness and awareness into what is for many of us a complicated and layered creative process. The following is a view of the creative process found in many meditative and contemplative art practices. Exploring this view can help us to further clarify our own view and expand our path of discovery.

Space, Form, and Energy

In essence, the creative process starts with nothing, and then something arises to become something, and lastly that some-thing communicates itself, and/or its inspiration. Ideally, what is communicated transcends the limitations of its form. Just as when we read a novel, the words we read create a whole world in our heads beyond the letterforms on the page. Similarly, a sculpture can evoke an experience beyond its composition, size, and shape.

The "nothing" we start with can be understood as no thing or no form. If you have nothing, all you have is empty space and that is where the creative process begins. It begins with *space*. Space is also referred to as "heaven" in some art forms, espe-cially ones that draw on ancient traditions like Asian calligraphy and painting, ikebana and kado (flower arranging practice), as well as many religious rites and dances. Today, at times, we can still benefit from seeing space as heaven. A thing, or anything, whether imaginary or real, possesses *form* and is the opposite of space. The ancient nomenclature for form would be "earth." That form could be quite solid like a bronze sculpture, or ephemeral like music, or anywhere in between.

During the creative process, ideas or inspirations arise out of a sense of spaciousness and then go through a process of formation, be it in the imagination as in pictures, or a relationship of shapes, sound, or movement, as examples. That ephemeral form is then given physical form through our art practice so others, as well as ourselves, can perceive and experience it. The final result becomes a vehicle for communicating the original inspiration, if not much more. By giving physical form to our inspiration, we are imbuing it with a sense of presence, and that presence can seem to have an *energy* or life of its own, what some call *élan vital*,[2] *ch'i*,[3] or *prana*,[4] breathing life into it so it communicates either itself or its inspiration. This principle is called *energy* or, in ancient times, "man."

> To transmit this quality of life (ch'i), the brush itself
> must be infused with spirit.

~ Diana Kan[5]

Whether these three principles are referred to as "space, form, and energy," or "heaven, earth, and man," they have been used to describe humanity's relationship to its environment since before written history. The oldest known representation of the three principles is a simple cross +. The horizontal line in the cross embodies the division between heaven and earth. The vertical line is the joining of heaven with earth by man.

Today these ancient principles are called by their less anthropomorphic names: space, form, and energy. They are used to describe the psychological manifestation of the creative process as well as the physical process. Although it is beneficial to see the physical and psychological aspects as separate manifestations, they are also like the waves and the ocean, and integral to one another within the creative process.

Space and Formlessness

The word "space" is used in several contexts. In formal meditation practice, space is the space we are practicing in. During our practice, when our mind and body are synchronized and we are awake and aware, we are in what I call "original space." Within the creative process as a meditation-in-action practice, the first principle, space, might appear physically as a blank canvas, an unused piece of paper, an empty stage, or an idle instrument. Psychologically, the principle of space would include nonthought, nonconceptual experience, or vision. Space is everywhere and so it is always the starting point for the creative process. You cannot create something if there is no space for it to arise and exist. For many of us, setting up an open space such as a studio takes less effort than bringing our minds to original space.

When we arrive at original space at the beginning of our creative process, we might find it calm and clear, or not. We might find ourselves bored, irritated, uncertain, bewildered, and even frightened. The uncomfortableness we experience seems to beckon self-consciousness and restlessness. Although this description of original space may sound uninviting, it is actually positive because it indicates that we are experiencing *space*. It can unsettle us because there are no clues to what will arise, or what we will do next. When people say they are blocked creatively, sometimes it's because the space they experience is uncomfortable and so they assume it's the wrong space. When we experience space with edginess, it is not because something is wrong but because space and our presence in it is charged. Something is about to happen.

Originality arises because we are open and we have not filled the space with habitual responses and mental activity. The challenge is to be in this psychological space and let go of any self-referencing hopes or fears that arise. And they will arise, but our practice is that, as soon as we recognize we are caught up in them, without self-criticism, we let go of them and simply return to original space. After all, every distraction is just another opportunity to practice returning to the object of meditation—which in this instance is our creative process.

When we start something new, the physical space we are facing is either empty or mostly empty. If we are returning to a work in progress, the space may no longer be empty, but it is still regarded as space even if there something in the physical space. Even if we started with a blank canvas as our space, there is still the canvas and whatever surface characteristics it may have. Psychologically, we start or return with a sense of spaciousness and inclusiveness. Physical and psychological space is all part of our original space. We may also come into our space with an inspiration, but that is also just part of our space. It only becomes something else when we are self-conscious about it and lose ourselves in self-dialoguing.

Whatever is included becomes part of the space and contributes to its uniqueness.

Wherever we are in our creative process, if we get lost or confused we know to come back and see what arises. Returning to original space does not mean that we stop our creative process and start completely over, or for that matter find a quiet place to meditate. It might turn out that is what we need to do, but we can first try the practice of meditation-in-action in which we come back fully to where we are. Sometimes it is useful to not only come back to our awareness of the environment, but the details of the environment as well. For example, if you are painting, it could be the brush in hand, the paint on its tip, the smell of the paint, the vibration of the canvas as the brush touches it. All the while, we have not lost track of the greater environment. There might be a dog barking, a phone conversation in the distance, and the sound of a plane flying way over our head. Just as heaven is still heaven even if we discover more stars, our whole environment is space. The space that we experience in our everyday life, as well as the creative process, is rarely empty.

When we are fully in original space, there is no separation between our state of mind and the physical space we find ourselves in. If we are on an empty stage, our mind is an empty stage; if we are before an empty canvas, our mind is an empty canvas. If the space is charged, we are energized, and if we are energized, the space is charged.

I find the Japanese concept of *ma* helpful. It translates as "an interval of time and space" and is used to indicate when more is going on than the apparently empty space. When it is used in the arts, it refers to a dramatic pause in theater, the space between the notes in a musical performance, and the open space in a painting or sculpture. It points us toward experiencing the space as not dull and boring, but alive and energetic.

Form Naturally Arises

We know from formal meditation practice that stuff, seemingly endless stuff, arises: inspiration as well as noise. Often so much noise is present that we cannot recognize what is inspiration. It is an accepted truth in physics that if an absolute vacuum could be produced in space, something would spontaneously arise within it: something out of absolutely nothing. It is the same with our psychological space. When we are confronted with spaciousness, many of us feel an almost irresistible tug to put something into it rather than wait and see what naturally arises from it. If we do arrive at original space, whether in formal meditation or our creative process, without immediately filling it with self-consciousness, something entirely different arises, something fresh and out of the ordinary.

Typically, we do fill the psychological space rather than wait. However, since it is only psychological space we are filling and not actual space, we can let go of all our imagined content and return to the space as it is. The simple awareness of our responses to space and spaciousness can be transformative. It can slow our responses down. It can quiet the noise. Our awareness alone can even dissolve it because awareness is a very powerful tool. It is awareness that allows us to perceive inspiration when it arises.

Remember, the type of meditation offered in this book is known as "mindfulness and awareness practice," also known by their ancient titles *shamatha* and *vipassana*. Shamatha is mindfulness practice, and it is translated as "calm abiding" or "peaceful-ness," because mindfulness leads to peacefulness. Vipassana is awareness practice and means "insight" because awareness leads to insight. Vipassana practice is the natural outgrowth of shamatha practice. Stuff is arising all the time in our minds, but it is our mindfulness practice that creates the space so we can perceive it as something less than a wall of noise. When we have prac-ticed mindfulness, we discover there is some space between our thoughts, and it is our awareness, our insight, that can perceive and distinguish inspiration from everything else. The way we develop awareness is by practicing mindfulness in order to arrive at the original space in which awareness blossoms.

We are practicing not only to arrive at or return to original space, but also to learn to *be* in it without manipulation. The sense of space is constant and all-encompassing, whether or not we are aware of it. After all, we exist in space, even though it often seems as though we are mentally trying to solidify every-thing to create a comfortable nest or cocoon for ourselves. Our mindfulness of our creative process as a meditation-in-action can help us to become more aware of space so we can be in space and be spacious enough to distinguish inspiration from our own uncomfortableness.

In addition to being aware of the psychological aspects of formation, there is the physical manifestation of form arising from space within the creative process. For example, a sudden inspiration might take form as a brushstroke on a blank canvas, the sketching out of the elements of a dance, the playing of a few notes for the first time, or typing out a few "first thoughts" that have arisen for a yet-to-be-written story. Since the psychological and physical aspects of formation are connected, something happens right at the moment the first mark, sound, or gesture is made. It is a kind of relief or release. But it is not because of some self-confirmation such as "I did it, I managed to fill the space with something and now I can relax and move on." It is more that our inspiration, which is surrounded by our mindfulness and awareness, has found a place to land and take shape. Its shape might even surprise or further inspire us. For some, it is the felt sense of uncertainty transforming into a glimmer of certainty and confidence.

Some type of relationship between original space and what might be called "original form" is taking shape, becoming an earth to a boundless heaven. It can be helpful to visualize the relationship of space and form in this way using the ancient terms of heaven and earth. Vast empty space becomes a heaven only when there is a planet, star, or galaxy to be seen within it. Whenever we stand on the earth and look to the sky, we have a felt sense of this relationship. The earth is comforting. Without the earth beneath us, our sense of being suspended in space would likely be disconcerting. With both space and form present, there is a felt sense of contrast, the certainty of a place to land, heaven and earth, yes and no, up and down, form and formless, silence and sound, ink and paper, and so our initial bewilderment seems to vanish.

There is the story of a Zen painter who asks his adept student to paint a picture of sky. The student picks up his brush but is confounded. How does one paint nothing as something? The master demonstrates by taking his brush and on a blank piece of paper paints a small solitary bird in flight. The bird transforms the space of the paper into an illustration of the sky.

Energy and the Cosmic Dance

Once the relationship between space and form is established, psychologically and physically, we can experience a kind of anti-climax because at this point it may be static. There is not much happening with space and form alone. Imagine a vast sky and an empty horizon. And yet we have an expectation, a curiosity about the relationship of space to form, heaven to earth, that invites, if not seduces, the next principle to manifest: energy. Energy is represented by man in ancient terminology. The physical mani-festation of the energy, or man principle, during the creation of a work of art is when a focus of interest is created, and the work seems to take on a life of its own. It's like lighting a candle in a darkened room.

One of the many possible examples of how we experience psychologically and physically the seduction of space and form is when a silence occurs in the middle of a conversation. We become very conscious of ourselves and the space between us. We feel more solid in ourselves and the space more empty in such moments. The pull to break the silence and say or do some-thing to bridge the gap can be irresistible and even feel painful. If we become too self-conscious, what seems to come out is our embarrassment. If we stay with the space between people, rather than collapse into ourselves or blurt something out, what arises is often spontaneous and genuine.

The same is true with our creative process. Every one of us comes to a place during a work in progress in which we don't know what comes next, or what it needs, or what it is calling out for us to do, or even not do. This is that awkward place where we are tempted to just think something up rather than stay with our felt sense and see what arises. We first experienced this type of the pull when we faced the principle of space in our creative process. What is different here is that we are now facing space *and* form, heaven *and* earth, and we are not drawn to fill something up, but to engage in some kind of dialogue or even *dance*. At this moment, it is important to recall the view that we are in a process of discovery rather than one of deduction.

Imagine for a moment you are dancing in harmony with your partner. You are not thinking about your next step because you know that, if you do, you may choke and crash into something. By regarding each moment of art-making as new, original space, we can be fully in touch and thereby responsive and spontaneous. It is by being in direct contact with original space and all that it comprises that we can discover what it is calling out for and how we can give our work presence—imbue it with a presence that others can experience: a presence that calls out to others to engage.

Psychologically, the energy principle can be seen as the discovery that we have something to present, express, and share with others. What's more, it can be a sense of joy and humor, which at its best, is insightful. The manifestation of the energy principle can also be found in the things that spark our curiosity or interest, tug on our hearts, or move our minds.

Seeing the energy principle as the man principle can be helpful. It is humanity that breaks the static relationship of heaven to earth. Imagine again a vast sky and unending horizon that is altered suddenly by the appearance of a being walking between them. Our attention is captured, we cannot help but look. The sense of absolute division of the first two principles, heaven and earth, has been profoundly changed into one that is dynamic because they are joined through a living figure on solid earth with spacious heavens above. Life, and the energy of life, are now present and if we are the observer, it draws us in to make our own relationship to it.

> It is to me the most exciting moment—when you have a blank
> canvas and big brush full of wet colour, and you plunge ...
> The knowing eye watches sharp as a needle; but the picture
> comes clean out of instinct, intuition and sheer physical
> action. Once the instinct and intuition gets into the brush-tip,
> the picture happens, if it is to be a picture at all.

~ D. H. Lawrence[6]

Space, Form, and Energy in Art

The principles of space, form, and energy, or heaven, earth, and man, appear universally in all forms of art and every creative endeavor. The greater our awareness of this, the more empowered we become to use these principles and appreciate them. A modern day example of the natural human articulation of the three principles can be seen in the Roden Crater project by artist James Turrell. Whether they were used consciously or not, it is a nearly literal manifestation of the principles of space, form, and energy, on a truly grand scale, which can be witnessed by visiting rodencrater.org.

Turrell has spent much of his life carving and reshaping the crater of a dormant volcano in northern Arizona, northeast of Flagstaff "into a celebration of light and space." The earth, or form principle, is literally the earth. When one enters the center of the crater and looks up at the sky from the middle of the bowl, there is a sense that the sky, heaven—or space—has been shaped into a solid dome. It is as if Turrell has made space as solid as the earth and earth space-like. The energy, or man, principle is the viewer's perception and experience, without which there would be no active principle. There is great power in the elegance and scale of this work.

Turrell's earlier works often used light alone to define the space of an interior environment. He accomplished this by projecting light within a room in a manner that created the illusion of another space within the room. Illumination became the principle of form, and like the Roden Crater project, our perception of it is the energy principle.

> *Turrell went even further, bypassing painting, sculpture*
> *and objects of any kind in making light itself his*
> *medium and human perception his subject ...*
> *He was learning about light and the unreliability of human*
> *perception, how we "make the world through our senses."*

> ~ Wade Graham[7]

Turrell's Roden Crater project is spectacular and readily lends itself to describing the principles of space, form, and energy in art. His light sculptures demonstrate that form does not have to be as solid as earth to convey shape and substance, and the energy principle can be as subtle as our own experience of the work. But what if your creative process and result is not as monumental in its simplicity in the sense of directness, but instead quite complex? Do these three principles limit the possibilities?

Complexity

Complexity and depth is, in fact, created by layering these principles. In other words, the space principle could have its own space, form, and energy within it, and form and energy could have their own three-fold principles. It is through this layering that as much complexity as you would like can be achieved. The three principles naturally flow or call out to us during our creative process when we are in tune with things as they are. As many art-makers find, the creative process is often a dialogue in which we first sketch things out, then take a fresh look, listen or feel and adjust, take another fresh view and add or subtract, but ultimately build toward the moment when it feels, looks, or listens "right." Whatever "right" is, it usually ocurrs when all three principles are present and in a relationship to one another that pleases, intrigues, or satisfies us in some way. The uniqueness of each work is determined by varying the emphasis of each principle in relationship to the other as well as to the layers, the subject matter, style of presentation, and choice of media. In this way, even though we start with merely three principles, we discover unlimited possibilities.

Intimacy with the Principles

As we come to appreciate these principles, they become a seamless part of our process. We are not thinking that we have completed the aspect of space and it is time to work on form. Rather, when we are in original space with our process, we feel the openness and spaciousness of space and its opposite—the density and solidity of form, and how they define each other, and whether or not there is any spark, life, and energy to what we are creating and communicating. Because we are in tune with our felt sense of these principles and our process, we naturally and spontaneously respond to what calls out to us, what invites us to participate. Maybe there is an invitation to yet another brushstroke, or a several more lines in a story, or a few more gestures in a performance. We respond as if in an unspoken dialogue. Our responses are as intimate and unselfconscious as lovers making love.

As we reexplore our work in progress and tune into our evolving original space, a thought sense naturally arises from the felt sense of viewing our results. Since that thought sense is so directly connected with our result, we know if that thought sense resonates with our perception of our results—as well as our inspiration—and we know whether any further action is invited. Maybe our inspiration has evolved as the work has, or maybe an auspicious accident occurs that leads us in a new direction and we are called to follow. Our thought sense can be extremely valuable in such moments because if our thought sense does not resonate with our perceptions, it can indicate that we may have tuned out our process or momentarily lost our connection to original space.

The creative process, as we will see more in the next chapter, is intimately involved with the viewing process in which we check in with our felt and thought senses to see if they resonate with one another and to explore what that may tell us about the work. The creative process is a process of creating *and* viewing. It is not so much a process of stepping back and scrutinizing our results, although you may wish to, but more of an ongoing awareness of what is being created, its felt sense, and whether or not any thought sense resonates with it. This takes place until our felt sense tells us it is time to stop and our thought sense agrees. We might stop because we find our results are true to our original inspiration or because they are not. It could even surprise and delight us to go beyond the inspiration or imaginative vision that we started with.

It is worth noting that these three principles also take shape in everyday life activities, including when we buy a new piece of furniture. We might have imagined where it should go in the space of our home, but we will not know if it works until after we physically place it. We know it is the right object in the right place when it comes alive within its surroundings, rather than being overwhelmed by them or standing apart from them.

Being able to identify these principles can help us spot what comes alive and what might have gone awry. Having a "perfect" idea or pure intent does not guarantee a satisfactory result. Sometimes what is created is less than desired regardless of our skills. When one of these principles feels too dominant or has too little presence, it can be felt. For example, we might discover that our work feels too solid and heavy-handed. Our felt sense is that it needs to lighten up, it seems to call out for more space or the introduction of some humor or irony. We can then make adjustments.

In truth, we have a felt sense of things all the time, but to benefit from this and go from direct experience to insight, we need to listen to the thought sense that arises from our felt sense and see if they resonate with one another.

Chapter Ten

The Viewing Process

The viewing process begins with "seeing things as they are." One of the perspectives meditative traditions offer is an explanation of how "seeing things as they are" takes place. It centers on the notion of a sixth sense, which is designated as the mind. The mind is where the other five sense experiences are gathered and rationalized into a complete perception. By rationalized, I mean when we hear the sound of a loud whistle, feel the ground tremble, and see an oncoming train, we put it all together as one experience. This is also a basic description of the viewing process, which is understood as more than just sight. The phrase "viewing process" is a convenience for what is actually a perceiving process that includes, to one degree or another, all our senses. If the artwork we perceive is music or poetry, our senses would be shifted more toward sound. If the volume is sufficient, the sound is felt as well as heard. In such a case our viewing process would be dominated by sound and touch. Regardless of the constellation of senses in use, if our perceptions remain unfiltered and undistorted, as happens when we allow our felt sense to naturally precede our thought sense and they are rooted in original space, then our sixth sense—mind—can "see things as they are."

The creative process works hand in hand with the viewing process. The viewing process, at its best, not only sees things as they are, it also provides invaluable information and feedback for the creative process. It is through the viewing process that, each time we look, we can take a fresh view and tune into our felt sense and then listen to our thought sense to see if it resonates. In this way, we come to know what needs to come next as well as when the creative process has ended and our work is finished.

Hearing What Art Has to Say

Art speaks to us. It is a conversation even when there are no words or thoughts. Art speaks to us while it is being created, and it speaks to us when it is a finished product. It sometimes speaks quietly and at other times, it shouts. Whenever we go to a performance, gallery, or museum, the viewing process provides the means to engage the art. Even though at times it may seem like a one-way conversation, there are interactive art forms that do change in response to us, our presence, our actions, and even our thoughts. Viewing art involves receiving what is being communicated.

When we have a conversation with another person, there are unspoken rules of engagement and we could say the same for art. Viewing art is not a passive process. When someone speaks to us, we are supposed to stop talking and listen in order to understand. If someone shows us a photo, even a vacation photo, we try to see what is in it and offer a response. And yet, some viewers attend an exhibition or performance and feel that showing up is all that is required. This is not true; the viewing process is an active form of engagement. It has its own discipline.

If we choose to perceive a work of art, we are choosing to take a fresh look by resting all of our available senses on it, including our mind, in order to feel it. To do so, we have to set aside our critical and often overstuffed minds for at least a brief moment and perceive what is there before employing analysis or evaluation. This may take some effort, especially if the art form is new to us or if we find it challenging to view or experience. But with our meditation practice, we know that it is possible to drop our storylines and self-dialoguing so we can come back to the moment. Viewing a work of art properly becomes just another form of meditation-in-action.

Obstacles to Viewing

Sometimes it can take the equivalent of a sensory atomic bomb to truly penetrate the wall of thoughts and mental activity in the viewer's attention. Some artists use outrageous and shocking imagery to grab the attention of a desensitized or disinterested public. Abject Art, art that is about revulsion and desire, uses this approach. Theoretically, once our attention is caught and our thoughts have slowed—if not momentarily stopped—the artist's message can then be communicated. However, too often what is communicated in this way becomes so tied up in the means of its shocking nature, the message is obscured. Often, the viewer does not bother to go beyond their shock to perceive the message.

I have known artists who, instead of resorting to such dramatic means, create art primarily for other artists, friends, and collectors: essentially, individuals who are educated about the artist's art or who have a prior knowledge of what is being communicated. When such artwork is presented to a public audience, their dealers and friends are left to explain it or simply market it as a commodity as if the artist were a brand name.

On one extreme end of the creative process, we can find heavy-handed art justified by the mistaken belief that the "shock of the new" is synonymous with originality. And, on the other end, if we see the viewing process as little more than passive observation, rather than contemplative observation, we cheat ourselves and undervalue the originality of the art. Such views inoculate us against a genuine experience of art. Due to previous poor experiences, many of us have become jaded and find it difficult to keep the pathway to experience of both felt and thought senses wide open. Staying open is no small task, even under ideal circumstances, because it requires that the viewer remain receptive to the widest spectrum of art. The viewer must be willing to accept challenging experiences as well as joyous ones because the erection of a filter for one involves placing a filter before everything.

We "think" art as much as, no, even more than, we "see" art.

~ Robert L. Solso[1]

Studies in cognitive science have shown how entrenched our viewing process is in our thought process. Scientists have compared the eye movements of those involved in the arts, such as artists and art historians, with those not involved in the arts as they viewed identical works of art. They discovered that those involved in the arts look at substantially less of the art. They focus on what they had been educated to look for. This was true whether or not the art was familiar. Artists and individuals with art training saw *less* because they had learned how to see only what they were supposed to see, and discarded what was "irrelevant." Viewers without formal training saw more because they did not know what they were supposed to see or to disregard.

Viewing as Meditation-in-Action

We have the physiological limits of perception, and then
we have this cultural overlay which is a learned perception.
They are not identical at all.

~ James Turrell[2]

To properly view art, we have to stop thinking "art." Instead, we need to directly perceive the work as it is without labels. When we get caught up in thoughts or ideas about the work, we need to bring ourselves back to an original space that includes the work. This involves a bit of patience because the moment in which we experience the work needs its own time. We will have all the time in the world to allow thoughts and critical thinking to come into play later. In truth, many art forms demand critical thinking to be fully appreciated, but for our experience to be reflective of the artwork rather than reflective of solely our thoughts, our thinking process must come after an unfiltered, direct experience.

Just as meditation requires practice, so does the viewing process. It is helpful to see it as a form of meditation-in-action. I have found in the many art salons and field trips I have offered that there are ways to facilitate the engagement of art based on the principles in this book. A salon involves a group inquiry and discussion of a particular principle, or art-related issue, in which we explore our thought and felt senses of a topic. It is facilitated by a volunteer in order to keep the group from drifting too far off the topic, as well as to encourage balance in the participation.

A field trip to view art would involve a guided viewing. The guidance is to help the group first identify our felt sense and then to see what thought sense arises from it. We make a point of writing down our thought senses. Writing them down documents our thought senses at the time so they can be referred to as opposed to recalled in later discussion. When written down right away, they retain greater potency because of their immediacy.

I like to choose works that participants are less likely to find familiar. I ask them not to call up their personal knowledge base and to avoid looking at any label or title for the work until they have had their own personal experience. This is all to encourage gathering as much of the felt sense of a work before engaging their thought sense. We then rest our senses on the product or performance. If it is a visual work such as a painting, I ask people to take a few moments to view the work from three different distances: close up, a little too far away, and finally a comfortable middle distance in which the art fills at least half our field of vision. Viewing a sculpture would include walking around it or through it, if possible. We are not trying to analyze anything; instead, we are being spacious and open, allowing ourselves to experience the totality of the piece. It is our openness and our spaciousness that will ultimately allow us to feel the various aspects of the work.

At this point, I find there are some questions we can ask ourselves to further clarify our felt sense while also drawing us deeper into the experience of the work. They involve using our felt sense of space, form, and energy as a means to tune into our perceptions and the work we are experiencing.

The first question is about space: *What about the work appears or feels spacious, if anything?* The Japanese principle of *ma* can sometimes play a role here when we ask ourselves: *What is the silent part?* This is particularly helpful with performances.

However, one of the most powerful experiences I have had of empty space in a contemporary work was Michael Heizer's *North, East, South, West:* four large sculptures of space cut deep into a concrete floor. When I stood nearby and looked down into the shaped holes in the ground, I felt the power and presence of the absence of something.

Participants write down what first thoughts come to mind when answering these questions. The process of tuning into our own experience and then trying to articulate that experience automatically generates our thought sense. We are not trying to think something up, but simply to respond with words. I have always found Alan Ginsberg's suggestion to, "Catch yourself thinking,"[3] helpful in moments like these. You are not trying to "put on the dog," as he would say, but rather "remember what you thought." The simple recollection of what pops up from immediate experience is often truest to the experience. It is often quite vivid. The thought sense that arises has a genuineness to it because it is based on our direct experience and is not a projection, story, or something imagined. If we find ourselves becoming lost in our thoughts, all we need to do is return to original space with all that it contains and re-ask ourselves what feels spacious in the work.

The words that arise can even be tested to see if they resonate with our experience in a way similar to the technique developed by Eugene Gendlin[4] called Focusing. In art-viewing, the originating experience is our interaction with the artwork, which gives rise to a first thought. When that thought is connected to our experience it will resonate. The activity of trying to identify what feels spacious generates words, phrases, and even complete sentences, but if we find ourselves getting involved in second, third, fourth thought and storyline or analysis, we should return to our original space: the work and our felt sense of it. If the artwork or performance is one we are familiar with, we have a bit more to do. We need to do our best to put that knowledge aside for several moments so we can perceive it with fresh senses and a fresh mind.

As we return to the viewing process after making our written notes about what feels spacious, we find our natural inquisitiveness takes us from one part of the art work to another. This can all take place very slowly or very quickly. As our senses increasingly take in more of the work, it literally takes shape in our mind as we are experiencing its form. We can provide additional focus for our engagement by exploring the felt sense principle of form.

We do so in the same way: by asking ourselves another question. *What feels solid?* In some works, it is more helpful to ask: *What grounds the space, what is the earth to its heaven?* As we articulate this felt sense, our thought sense takes shape. We can write that down as well. Once again, our thought sense, our words, can be tested for resonance with our felt sense.

Our third inquiry is to ask ourselves what tugs on us, seduces our interest, or moves us. It can also be what repels us or sets us on fire. All are aspects of the energy principle. The principle of space is frequently what stops our mind by short circuiting the constant stream of thoughts. When our thoughts are confronted with such space, they seem to evaporate like a droplet in the heat of Death Valley. In contrast, the principle of energy is what moves our mind, or what is referred to as heart/mind in many meditative traditions. The energy principle also manifests as the recognition and realization that something is being communicated and that we have received it. In the same way random words assemble themselves into a sentence and a meaning is born, our initial felt sense grows into an experience that manifests as a realization, an appreciation, and possibly an epiphany. Tolstoy described it as an infection.[5] Our mind and being are energized by the artwork. A powerful work of art can feel like an open invitation for the viewer to dance and play with the energy it communicates.

At this point, any knowledge we possess can be brought into play and it will serve to enrich and deepen our experience, as well as encourage us to further explore the artwork. Layer after layer can unfold. Because all great art has these three principles of space, form, and energy built one upon the other—whether by design or auspicious accident—we are drawn to view and review, experience and reexperience them as if they are fountains nourishing our very being.

If we choose to, we can extend our engagement by asking ourselves three more contemplative questions: *What do we feel the work represents? What do we feel the work expresses? How do we feel it accomplishes what it does?* Viewing artwork in terms of what it represents, if anything; what it expresses, if anything; and formal issues are classical ways of exploring art. If we adopt this method after we have had an opportunity to have our own felt and thought sense of what we are viewing, it turns what might ordinarily be an intellectual or historical exercise into an expanded personal experience.

Viewing with Knowledge

For much of the history of art, art was representational. The art consisted of recognizable images and scenes that represented either a historical or spiritual event, or sometimes both. In viewing such a work of art, we might ask ourselves to express what we feel is being represented and find that it feels like it is mostly surface, or signage, in that it is primarily telling a story. On the other hand, we might feel that even though it is depicting a story it still embodies, or evokes, something in us and so it has a strong felt sense, substance, or symbolism to it. The very attempt to articulate this, especially by writing it down, gives rise to our thought sense of its representation.

Historically, artistic expression of feelings over ideas came much later than representation. Many say this occurred during the time of romanticism, which began in the latter part of the 18th century. Notwithstanding, exploring art in terms of what it expresses, as well as what it represents, helps us to expand our view and deepen our appreciation. By directing our attention to the felt sense of what is being expressed, we open ourselves to experiencing it as opposed to dispassionately identifying it. If we are looking for a readily identifiable art form that attempted to rouse our felt sense over our thought sense, it would be German Expressionism. Even though many of the works of that time were allegories, or had stories that accompanied them, their power manifests in what we feel when we view them. When we engage such works and ask ourselves what we feel, we begin to approach what they express.

Formalism is a third view that arose with Modern art. Formalism refers to the formal qualities of a work of art: the size, shape, appearance, colors, texture, and their relationship to one another. Form takes precedence over content, or we could say the form *is* the content. The later works of Piet Mondrian, as well as those by contemporary artists like Don Flavin and Richard Serra are graphic examples of this style. When we ask ourselves how we feel a work communicates itself, we are asking: *What is the felt sense of each of its formal qualities?* This third view is helpful because it enables us to include works of art that do not appear to represent anything, or express anything. Instead, they are about the relationship of one form to another and what felt and thought sense they evoke.

It is possible to go further and ask questions about style, specific content, intent of the artist, and so on, first experiencing our felt sense and then the thought sense that subsequently arises. In a field trip, at this point in the viewing process someone reads the title of the work, the name of its author, and a few paragraphs of readily available information regarding the work and the artist. After that, we return to original space, which now includes not only the work of art, but our knowledge of it. We then take a fresh and newly informed view, alternately dropping the information and then letting it come into play to see if it resonates with our experience as we reexplore our felt sense of its space, form, and energy. We then share our experiences by reading examples of what we wrote for each inquiry. The reason we read out loud is so we do not edit ourselves based on the words of others.

By sharing our experiences in this way, we receive the most expansive view possible of the work. In such field trips, inexperienced viewers find they do not need to be art historians or museum curators to gain a profound appreciation of the art they view. Experienced viewers find they can trust their gut sense and feel a work of art as much as "think it." All seem to find that reviewing art in this manner is an enriching process. Each successive viewing is not merely to reexperience the same, but an opportunity for further discovery, to become more inclusive of other viewpoints.

Benefitting from Others' Viewing Experiences

This viewing process is applicable to our own art work. To know if the art we make is communicating anything at all, we must be able to view our results as our audience will. However, our familiarity with our work can be a powerful obstacle to taking a fresh look. In recognition of this, we may seek feedback—preferably independent feedback. The typical sources are friends and colleagues who wish to be supportive and from whom we tend to seek support—which can lead to trouble. They could be too kind and gentle or offer little feedback to work with. More trouble can arise when we are looking for self-confirmation rather than information. If there is a desire for self-confirmation or an ego massage, we will tend to edit and distort the feedback to fit our measure of self-esteem. Whether we take the gift of unwarranted praise or dismiss a negative and unpalatable response, the result is the same: inaccurate or inaccurately perceived feedback.

When self-confirmation is removed from the equation—and this is not an easy task—feedback is just feedback. It is information, pure and simple. If we find that someone does not "get" what we are attempting to communicate, our first response is to listen even more carefully and ask more questions, as opposed to looking to blame or for a defense. The message, no matter how it is packaged, could be that we simply did not do our job well enough. Maybe we failed to stop their mind or move their heart. It is not the viewer's job to figure out why and how there is an unbridgeable gap between our efforts and their experience. That is the job of the art's creator.

To receive feedback in the most constructive way possible, we need to practice listening before hearing, as if we are scientists performing a test and measuring the results before drawing conclusions. When we hear before listening, we cherry-pick that which confirms our agendas, and in so doing distort the feedback. To grasp the truth of our predicament, we must be able to listen to feedback in as unbiased a way as possible.

Integrating the principles of space, form, and energy into one's creative and viewing processes might feel awkward in the beginning. Today, the use of perspective in drawing and painting is taken for granted. We are so used to seeing perspective applied that we only notice it when it is "off." Yet, when we look at the entire history of art, the use of perspective is a relatively recent invention. When it was first invented as a tool some five hundred years ago, it was considered truly magical. As we learn to perceive and use principles like space, form, and energy, they might feel as formulaic as when we first learned how to use perspective. But as we work with them, the principles become integrated into our awareness and become a seamless part of our activities as a tool that naturally and accurately describes our reality.

Chapter Eleven

Conditional and Unconditional Beauty

Is beauty solely in the eye of the beholder or is it physically present in an object of beauty? Why should we care? Let's start an investigation with a definition of beauty and see where it leads.

> *Beauty: A characteristic or combination of characteristics affording great sensory pleasure.*
>
> ~ *Merriam-Webster*[1]

We could simplify this: *Beauty is that which gives pleasure to the senses.* How does this notion of beauty connect to art-making and art-viewing? One definition of art makes that connection.

> *Art: the conscious production or arrangement of sounds, colors, forms, movements, or other elements in a manner that affects the sense of beauty.*
>
> ~ *Houghton-Mifflin*[2]

There is a curious phrase in this definition: "affects the sense of beauty." It does not appear to refer to a literal sense organ like one of the five sense organs that biologists refer to. I believe it's reasonable to assume it is referring to an experience. If so, how does that experience occur?

119

According to the *Abhidharma*, there are *six* senses. As mentioned in a previous chapter, the first five are the same as those in Western science. The sixth sense is mind, with the function of integrating the other five senses and the information they offer into a complete experience.

The *Abhidharma* teachings use the Sanskrit term *citta* to refer to mind. Citta is the totality of mental processes and manifestations and is equated with the thinking, discriminating mind.[3] The mind makes sense of the senses. Mind is where the "sense of beauty" occurs rather than at the individual sense receptors: eyes, ears, tongue, skin, and nose.

If there was no sixth sense such as mind to process our sensory input, then we would not connect the sound of someone talking with seeing them speak. Studies at the California Institute for Technology[4] in cognitive science have shown how dependent one sense is on another to compose an experience. Our mind not only cognizes what the other five senses sense, it can also create its own understanding of what is perceived. An everyday example of this is when we see someone suddenly grimace in pain and we mirror that by grimacing as if we are in pain. Another example is when someone vividly describes a taste we are familiar with and we salivate while imagining tasting it. The actual experience is not the same as the imagined one, but mirroring studies show our brains are attempting to recreate the experience.

Knowing that the mind perceives and also invents and projects does not help us to answer the question of whether beauty is perceived or invented by the mind. Not knowing whether the experience of beauty is a thought or a perception raises another important, fundamental question: *Exactly what are we working with when we are making or viewing art? Are we working with an idea or a felt presence?* Some have argued that art is just an idea or a concept and we don't need to make anything. If we do make something, it is only a reference point for the idea. The investigation of beauty leads us to some of the most fundamental questions regarding the nature of our experience and what generates it. Is there a physical reality that exists outside our mind or is it all just taking place in our mind?

The question of the nature of beauty, as well as the implications of it, have made any discussion of beauty and aesthetics a treacherous endeavor. Many philosophers through the ages have tried to elucidate beauty and seemed on solid ground until another philosopher refuted their assertions. With such a history, it would seem wise to avoid such a discussion, and so many of us do. But if we are exploring the nature of the creative and viewing processes, it is impossible to sidestep. Any road that leads to understanding what makes art, art, seems to pass right through "the sense of beauty." To me, it has always seemed an intractable discussion. It was not until I brought a meditative practitioner's perspective to this dialogue that it seemed possible to get beyond simply arguing the polar opposites.

Discussions of beauty tend to center on two opposing positions: a subjective view that beauty is in the eye of the beholder and an objective view that beauty is universal and present in the object of beauty regardless of the viewer's ability to perceive it. This dispute rests in part on the stance that the subjective view and the objective view are antinomies, two rational positions that contradict one another, which implies that we must choose between them.

Because in their common usage the terms "subjective" and "objective" are antagonistic and dualistic, a discussion of beauty might prove more fruitful if the terms "conditional" and "unconditional" were substituted. These terms are often used by contemplative and meditative traditions. They are less dualistic and even more descriptive by referring to conditions or the lack of them.

Conditional, like subjective, is dependent on causes and conditions and refers to the relative nature of things. Unconditional, like objective, is independent of causes and conditions and refers to an absolute.

Conditional Beauty

The view that beauty is solely in the eye of the beholder asserts that beauty is temporal and relative to our learning, culture, and personality—and is therefore conditional. This view was strongly asserted by the English poet and critic, I. A. Richards in his book *Practical Criticism* in 1929.[5] Although quite modern with regard to world history, the text is considered an early Western work on criticism and its psychological root. If this view comprises the whole truth of beauty, then it would follow that the definition of beauty would be mutable and readily influenced by whoever controls the culture. Our world history reflects some who took this view to the extreme. The Nazis attempted to control their culture and view of what is beautiful by declaring that certain art was degenerate and art that supported their political aesthetic was Aryan, beautiful, and good. Mao, the Taliban, and others throughout history have followed this path, believing that if you change the definition of what is beautiful, you will have changed the perception of the thing itself.

War is peace.
Freedom is slavery.
Ignorance is strength.

~ George Orwell[6]

The view that beauty is solely in the eye of the beholder also implies that the characteristics which give pleasure to the senses are not present in the object. Instead, they are conscious or unconscious projections overlaying the object and what is perceived is our own sensibility reflected back to us—that gives us pleasure. In this view, if we stopped projecting, beauty would, by definition, disappear and what would be left would elicit no pleasure. One of the false fears about meditation is that if meditation practice is successful, attachments will dissolve until we no longer care about anything. What gave us pleasure or held meaning for us will no longer. But in truth, what does dissolve is the neurotic grasping—not the caring.

The relative view, in which beauty is a mental construct alone, is easily tested against direct experience. There are several ways to a direct, unfiltered, nonself-referencing experience, but one of the most consistent and effective paths is to develop a mindfulness and awareness meditation practice. It works to synchronize our mind and body, relax our relentless self-dialoguing, and ground ourselves in the present moment and environment. In such moments of direct experience, we are wakeful and aware, and we can glimpse things as they truly are—as opposed to how we imagine they are. In such meditative moments, our senses do not stop working. They are actually heightened, and any pleasure they transmit does not cease because we have stopped thinking. We are still conscious and aware of our senses and what does or does not give them pleasure.

What we discover for ourselves is that self-referencing, self-dialoguing, and maintaining some thought stream about beauty is not required to experience pleasure and actually gets in the way. With direct perception, we realize for ourselves that what gives pleasures to the senses, beauty, is not a projection.

Unconditional Beauty

Immanuel Kant asserted that beauty was not dependent on purpose or utility and the experience of it induced moments of "disinterested pleasure." The implication is that there is something inherently present that anyone can discover and our experience of it is free from prejudging and self-interest. Kant's view has held up over time to the point where it is commonly found in dictionaries as a second definition of beauty.

> *Beauty: Perfection that excites admiration or delight for itself rather than for its uses: a quality in a consummate thing that induces immediate and disinterested pleasure.*
>
> ˜ Merriam-Webster[7]

This notion of disinterested pleasure, a pleasure not based on our self-interest, prejudice, or projection, appears to recognize the sense of unconditional beauty found in contemplative art traditions.

> *Fundamentally, art is the expression of unconditional beauty, which transcends the ordinary beauty of good and bad.*
>
> ˜ Chögyam Trungpa Rinpoche[8]

For unconditional beauty to transcend the values of good and bad found in conditional beauty, it would have to exist beyond the limitations of the eye of a single viewer. Unconditional beauty is perceived from an unconditional, transcultural, or naked view in which everything is inherently beautiful by way of its very existence, including what we might otherwise see as repulsive. Unconditional beauty is a discovery rather than a projection.

Beauty—be not caused—It Is—

~ Emily Dickinson[9]

Unconditional beauty is like the sun that illuminates all equally. Conditional beauty in no way contradicts unconditional beauty and vice versa. Conditional beauty is the various relative manifestations of unconditional beauty. The sun may illuminate all without discrimination, but that does not mean a caterpillar is the same as a maggot, and depending on our culture and style we might consider one to be more or less beautiful. The more we allow our relative acculturation to interact with our perceptions, the more we increase the conditioning of our experience of beauty and thereby limit and alter it. If we allow it, conditioning can increase to the point at which we completely lose sight of the underlying connection: unconditional beauty. However, losing sight of it does not mean it has disappeared.

From a conditional point of view, beauty and ugliness are opposites. Beauty gives pleasure to our senses and ugliness makes us uncomfortable. From an unconditional point of view, when we are not editing or judging our experience, beauty and ugliness at their root are the same because they are both about *sensation*.

125

Art and Everyday Life

This leads us to wonder, if the underlying experience is about sensation, then what is the difference between the sensations of everyday life experience and the aesthetic experience? Is everyday life art, or is art everyday life? This also has been one of the great unresolved issues of modern Western philosophy: understanding the differences and similarities between the aesthetic experience and the experience of everyday life.

Our experience of art and everyday life does seem to be different, and yet similar. From a conditional point of view they are different, and from an unconditional point of view they are not different. This is not a problem or a contradiction. This is because the relationship between conditional and unconditional is symbiotic. They inform each other and define each other, just as space defines form and form defines space. If one did not exist the other would have no meaning at all.

Conditional and unconditional beauty are not competitive views, even though our conditional minds—when presented with two things—automatically begin to judge which is better, which is right and which is wrong. When confronted with conditional and unconditional beauty, some of us might favor the latter because it can be seen as somehow grander with its overarching view that transcends cultural notions of what is beautiful and what is ugly. Others might choose conditional beauty, rejecting the other as too abstract and impractical because despite any unconditional experience we may have, it is quickly personalized and made conditional anyway.

Nevertheless, understanding the conditional is only possible because of unconditionality. This principle of mutual inclusivity or interdependence was shared by and became a foundation for the two great schools of Buddhist philosophy, *Madhyamika* and *Yogachara*. The truth of conditionality and the truth of unconditionality, also known as the "two truths," are as opposite as two sides of a coin and as inseparable. The one side of the coin we view at any moment cannot be used as an argument to deny the existence or validity of the other side. It is merely what we perceive at the moment until we look at the other side or come to realize its totality as a coin. If we can come to see the two truths of beauty as one totality and apply that to art-making and -viewing, we can begin to notice that many works of art play with our sensibility regarding one or both types of beauty.

Some works of art appear more focused on conditional beauty, such as traditional paintings of still life and landscapes by artists like Pieter Brueghel the Elder, Fredric Edwin Church, and John Peto. Others, like the works of the Color Field painters from the 1940–80s, like Mark Rothko, Clyfford Still, Sam Francis, Ed Moses, and Ingrid Calame, seem dedicated to unconditional beauty in that they are without any recognizable form.

Regardless of their respective emphasis in a work of art, when conditional and unconditional beauty are working in concert what is communicated has the potential to cut through a viewer's conditionality, language, and cultural boundaries. One example of the two truths of beauty working in concert is visible in the friendly competitiveness of Picasso and Matisse. There are books, exhibits, and even websites devoted to their exchanges. They maintained a visual dialogue by creating works of art in response to each other's paintings. Much of that dialogue had to do with the two truths of beauty.

Matisse is about achieving a meditative, rare, sublime beauty with everything he does. Picasso is about being savage and masculine and psychological and peering mercilessly inside his own head and looking at what it is to be sexual or to be old or to be dying or to be still feeling OK and full of beans.

~ Matthew Collings[10]

Collings uses Matisse's *Odalisque with Tambourine*, 1926, and Picasso's response, *Nude in a Red Chair*, 1929, to make his point. Matisse's painting is imbued with and evokes a strong sensuality. On a conditional scale, to many around the world, it possesses great beauty especially when compared to *Nude in a Red Chair*, Picasso's shockingly ugly parody of Matisse's painting. It has been said that Picasso's goal was to question the whole notion of what is beautiful and what is ugly. He challenged the conditionality of beauty. The manner in which Picasso painted the work also exudes sensuality—if not beauty—albeit in an uncomfortable way, even today. What results is a beautifully painted, ugly figure of a woman. He is challenging us to see ugly as beautiful, or to see through our conditional notions to an unconditional vision. Can we see through the wildly distorted naked figure of a woman with flying pendulous breast and vagina and anus on the same picture plane, to a masterfully painted composition of shapes and brilliant colors that compel us to look and feel?

It would seem that Matisse, the sensualist who painted while dressed in a fine business suit, wanted us to feel something and not think so much about it; Picasso, the unconventional intellectual in a T-shirt and beret, wanted us to think about what we felt. At the same time, their emphasis of one aspect of beauty over the other in their individual works is not the denial of the other.

The two painters actually liked each other's work and collected it. Matisse's art is not dumb and merely decorative, and Picasso's could never be taken for passionless. Their differing styles help us see and feel the interplay of our knowledge and experience, our thought sense and felt sense. When we experience the felt sense and thought sense of their works, we are tested to see and experience ugliness as beautiful, and if we can, we arrive at the ever-present doorway to glimpsing unconditional beauty.

In some ways we can use logic, our thought sense, to lead us to the doorway and even crack it open. But logic alone is too limited to take us all the way into the experience. We could also wait patiently for a chance spontaneous moment in which we find ourselves at an open doorway. Or we could develop the kind of mindfulness and awareness found in meditative disciplines—and, to a degree, also found in artistic disciplines—in order to walk through that doorway into the experience of unconditionality.

Exploring the Totality of Experience

Centuries before the Matisse–Picasso rivalry, the Buddhist art of the Himalayas required practitioners of meditation to perceive unconditionally. The tradition depicts both exquisitely peaceful deities and terrifyingly ugly ones as embodiments of aspects of enlightened mind and enlightened action. The 17th and 18th century examples below are relatively recent when you consider representations of them date back to at least the 8th century.

White Tara is the female deity of compassion, who is white in color because she embodies the purity, pacifying, and healing qualities of compassion. Her right hand is turned outward as an act of generosity and her left hand is holding the stem of a white lotus flower, which suggests enlightenment. She exudes the attractiveness and sensuousness of a beautiful young woman. Her jewelry represents the perfection of six transcendent actions: discipline, patience, energy, generosity, meditation, and knowledge. The five jewels in her crown each represent one of the five wisdoms: the wisdom of equanimity, mirror-like wisdom, the wisdom of discriminating awareness, the wisdom of all-accomplishing action, and the wisdom of all-encompassing space. Her expression is not unlike a Madonna painted by Leonardo da Vinci, one of serenity and loving kindness. Every facet of this work has significance, but it is all composed to evoke a sense of beauty and tranquility in everyone who views it.

Figure 8: *White Tara, a Buddhist deity of peaceful compassion*

In the other extreme, we have Palden Lhamo, also a female deity of compassion. She is so terrifying and frightfully ugly that Christian missionaries, who traveled to the Himalayas around the time of Matisse and Picasso, saw such images as disgusting representations of demons and destroyed them whenever and wherever possible. Palden Lhamo has three bloodshot eyes, vampire teeth, and wears freshly severed heads for a necklace, five dry skulls as a crown, a shawl of human skin, a tiger skin skirt, and holds in her right hand a skull cup containing urine, puss, semen, and blood. All scary stuff indeed. What could the makers of such a work be thinking when they created such an outrageous art form?

Figure 9: *Palden Lhamo, a Buddhist deity of wrathful compassion*

Was their intent similar to Dante's when he wrote *Inferno*—using imagery to scare us into becoming believers? Is Palden Lhamo like the Western demon from hell who will torture us for our sins? Certainly not to anyone who is a meditative practitioner in the tantric tradition. Instead, such imagery embodies that aspect of the truth that is terrifying, torturously painful, and totally outrageous. As many say, the truth may set us free, but it can be a hellish path to freedom.

If we take an informed view of this figure, we understand that the third eye represents the ability to see wisdom as unfiltered and unconditional in all its forms. The garland of severed heads signifies the cutting off of mental confusions, and the five-skull crown is the transmutation of the five poisons—passion, aggression, ignorance, pride, and jealousy—into the five wisdoms. The skull cup of blood and excrement represents the medicine we need to transform our madness into sanity. The shawl of human skin indicates the adornment of selfless compassion. In Palden Lhamo's right hand is a trident that can pierce the heart of passion, aggression, and ignorance in one blow. Every aspect of this iconography embodies the felt and thought senses of wrathful compassion. Such imagery is asking more of us than to just see ugly as beautiful in terms of aesthetics, but to perceive the wisdom of seeing beyond conditionality in every aspect of our existence.

Joining Conditional Beauty and Unconditional Beauty

We started by asking whether beauty is solely in the eye of the beholder or if something is inherently present in an object we experience. But as we have explored, beauty cannot be solely in

132

the eye of the beholder since it is only one side of the coin. Beauty is in the eye of the beholder *and* present in the object itself. If we are in tune with our environment as well as ourselves, we experience an object's presence first and then we condition it to our own mind's eye. Because of this, we can have two people share an experience and spontaneously agree that something is beautiful, and yet when they explain the "what" and the "why," it can be for different reasons.

Through the practice of mindfulness and awareness meditation, we empower ourselves to glimpse unconditionality. Experiencing beauty in such moments makes the work of art unconditionally beautiful. Even so, we eventually personalize it and make it conditional. The lesson here is not that we are somehow doomed to fall back into conditionality and lose sight of unconditionality and that this is a bad thing. Rather, it is because we have had a glimpse of unconditionality that we can learn to see through our conditioning to the unconditional whether we are meditating or engaging in meditation-in-action. This provides the opportunity to perceive both types of beauty in art-making and -viewing at any time.

Is the perception of the two types of beauty a separate experience, simultaneous, or sequential? It depends. It is a bit like sign and symbol in that the perceptions are inseparable and always present when the other is. They manifest in a matter of degree, according to what is being presented to us, and within the context of what we bring to the experience. Being able to perceive the two beauties also provides the basis to glimpse what others might perceive as beautiful or not and so expand our own boundaries and appreciation.

Why should we care about beauty and its two types? Because exploration of them brings us not only to the essence of art-making and art-viewing, but the very nature of things as they are and our relationship to them. It also leads us to see through ourselves to a common ground and celebrate the wealth of experiences of others.

Chapter Twelve

Presence and the Sublime

*Nothing redeems but beauty, its generous permission,
its gorgeous celebration of all that
has previously been uncelebrated.*

~ Dave Hickey[1]

*Beauty is an ecstasy: it is as simple as hunger.
There is really nothing to be said about it. It is like the
perfume of a rose: You can smell it and that is all.*

~ William Somerset Maugham[2]

*Beauty is unbearable, drives us to despair,
offering us for a minute the glimpse of an eternity that we
should like to stretch out over the whole of time.*

~ Albert Camus[3]

"Redemption," "gorgeous celebration," "ecstasy," "unbearable," and "despair." All powerful reactions to the experience of beauty. Could it be that in the absence after its presence we are driven to appreciate beauty so and despair at its loss? Imagine a life without beauty. What is going on during the experience of beauty that makes us feel so much and wax so poetic? We could replace the word "beauty" in each quote with the word "love" as if the two were interchangeable. It is as if these authors are describing a love affair with their sensory experience.

Beauty in Pain and Pleasure

Let us explore the experience of beauty in light of our experience of meditation and see where it leads. To begin with, the measure of any experience depends on the degree in which our mind and body are synchronized with each other and the environment. If our mind, the sixth sense, is not attentive to the other five senses, we cannot expect to experience much beyond our thoughts. With physically painful experiences, disengaging from our five senses might appear beneficial. There are forms of meditation that teach how to disengage from our senses and create a kind of mental pleasure. However, they are problematic because being disconnected, possibly even deluded, is the opposite of what is required during the creative and viewing processes.

Mindfulness and awareness meditation practice strengthens our connection to our environment through our senses. It encourages us to completely open up without reservation or discrimination. It invites us to be more than participants in our world—it offers us the opportunity to be one with it. Here and earlier, I have used this phrase: "one with." Such oneness happens when we drop our self-referencing and self-dialoguing and experience a sense of wholeness with our mind and body and environment. Meditators and others engaged in various forms of spirituality refer to this experience as "nonduality." In such moments, the sense of I and other dissolves into oneness.

The explanation of oneness or nonduality can sound almost technical. But what I am talking about is simply an expansion of an analogy I used earlier of two lovers. Only now they are so entwined that they can no longer tell where one of them ends and the other begins. In many meditative traditions, the mind is referred to as heart/mind and it is located in the chest rather than the head. Some traditions include a devotional aspect to their meditation practice as a means to relax a potentially over-intellectualized mind, as well as to encourage us to become one with our world. This happens because we are in love.

The nondual experience occurs when we are no longer watching ourselves having an experience: we are the experience. Our senses are without filters and we experience heightened clarity because the boundary between ourselves and our environment has dissolved. Such connectedness inevitably leads to a vivid experience, in which we are not only experiencing pleasure more deeply, but also pain more sharply. We cannot help it, because all the ways that we habitually anesthetize ourselves—in a sense, keep our world at an even, comfortable temperature—have evaporated for a moment. The key here is that any filter we use to mitigate the painful experiences affects pleasurable experiences as well. If we wish to truly experience all the beauty and pleasure the world has to offer, we cannot dull or shut ourselves off from the painful parts. We may be able to steer away from them, but we cannot ignore them when they present themselves. Camus's words recognize that beauty can lead us to great heights and also to despair. But at the same time, has not such a truth been the inspiration of many great works? Painful experiences can serve to open us up and inspire us to be creative.

Resonance with an Object

Experiencing beauty is a process of "extending the mind through the sense perceptions."[4] When our sense perceptions are in direct contact with the object of beauty and our mind is attentive, then our mind and body naturally begin to synchronize, resonate, and harmonize with the object. The pleasure we experience during such an encounter is a likely result of our resonance with the object.

I will connect this experience with the principles of space, form, and energy discussed in the chapter on the viewing process. Whatever the object is—a performance, an environment, a painting, or a novel—it shares its presence through its unique conflation of space, form, and energy. Just as the object possesses the three principles, so do we. During the process of observation, our mind and its openness can be seen as the principle of space. Our body and what it senses is the principle of form. Whatever the object communicates to us is the energy principle. Our mind, body, and what is communicated can become so synchronized with the object of beauty that we begin to resonate with its incarnate spaciousness, solidity, and energy as if we were in sexual or spiritual union with it.

Simply put, the rituals of "aesthetic" submission in our culture
speak the language so closely analogous to those of sexual
and spiritual submission that they are all but
indistinguishable when conflated in the same image.

~ Dave Hickey[5]

Hickey points out that the words used to describe great beauty and the act of submitting to the experience are often indistinguishable from those used to describe spirituality and sexual union. When we are experiencing a work of great beauty, it is as if we are locked in an intimate embrace that affords great sensory pleasure. In great works of art, the three principles of space, form, and energy are working in concert and on multiple levels even when the work might appear simple. If we allow ourselves to thoroughly experience the work by synchronizing with it on as many levels as it may offer, we can experience a powerful, intimate felt presence.

Ch'i and Felt Presence

The notion of *presence* is not often found within definitions of art or in descriptions of the characteristics that make art, art. Skill, intellect, intuition, communication, and aesthetics are fairly common in Western literature, although usually not found all together in one definition. Hsieh-Ho,[6] a painter and critic during the 6th century who lived in Nanking, wrote the *Six Canons of Art*. He could be seen as one of the earliest people to refer to a sense of presence in art through his use of the term *ch'i*. He incorporated the Chinese term ch'i into his first and most important canon. Whereas the other five canons had to do with discipline and technique, the first canon—on which all the others depended— was about what cannot be learned but only discovered through an intuitive process.

The first canon is called *ch'i yun sheng tung*, which translates literally as "spirit rhythm life movement."[7] Western scholars have often found this phrase confusing and have sought to visually identify or locate this principle in Asian art, not unlike a neurosurgeon dissecting the brain in an attempt to find the mind. But the first canon is about what is felt, a felt presence, rather than what is seen or thought. For the artist, it is about infusing their work with ch'i. This is not easy to do, but to Hsieh-Ho it is what distinguishes a work of art.

Ch'i literally means "air," "vapor," "breath," "ether," or "energy," and it refers to the vital energy or life force that pervades and enlivens all things.[8] When we experience this energy or life force, we sense it as a presence. In the Hindu tradition it would be *prana*, which means "the breath of life." You can find in the writings of Henri Bergson, an influential French philosopher of the first half of the 20th century, this notion of *élan vital*, life force.

All these terms are used in part to describe a work of art that has "a life of its own," or a performer who has "stage presence." I suspect that we have all met people, experienced performances, and seen or created a work of art and have felt a particularly powerful sense of presence. It is this quality that Hsieh Ho is calling our attention to. Through his first canon, Hsieh Ho proclaims that for something to be art it *must* have this quality. It has to have a life of its own beyond the sum of its materials and the person who created it.

Harmony in the Creative Process

When I am in my painting, I'm not aware of what I'm doing ... the painting has a life of its own. I try to let it come through. It is only when I lose contact with the painting that the result is a mess. Otherwise there is pure harmony ...

~ Jackson Pollock[9]

Pollock's quote illustrates this notion of a work of art having a life of its own, and also points out that in order to invest it with such life our creative process must be unselfconscious and in harmony. Because we are not burdened by ourselves, we can attune to the living quality emerging from the art itself and observe the ch'i as it arises, evolves, becomes more potent, and takes on a life of its own. Just as spontaneity requires us to be tuned into our senses and our world, we must also tune in to experience true harmony, presence, or ch'i.

Some people associate harmony with a kind of do-nothing, fuzzy, slow-motion, bucolic-like happy existence. That is one kind of harmony. Unfortunately, it is generally achieved by stupefying ourselves and surrendering much of our intelligence. It is the opposite of what I am discussing—harmony based on wakefulness and awareness, which is intelligent, alive, and energetic. It is about a kind of interconnected dynamism. It's analogous to the forces in an atom, quantum mechanics, or string theory in which apparently opposing, neutral, and attractive forces are all in constant motion—changing, giving and taking, and yet in total harmony.

We have been talking primarily about harmony and wakefulness within the creative process, but there is also the harmony that we may experience on viewing our results or that of others. This gives rise to two questions. If we are art-makers who work with some intention, do we wish to create works that we alone harmonize with, or ones that others may harmonize with as well? In either instance, are we trying to energize and wake ourselves up as well as others, or merely anesthetize and put all to sleep?

Incorporating the Enriching Presence of Yün

There is another ancient term, *yün*, which can be helpful here because it describes a particular type of presence, one that offers harmony and resonance.

*The Chinese character yün can mean organic harmony,
concord, charm, resonance, or rhythm. When ch'i and
yün function together as a single term, the term refers
to the vital breath of harmony,
incorporating the meanings of both characters.*

~ Wucius Wong[10]

When a work of art possesses "the vital breath of harmony"
and we tune in to it and allow our ch'i and yün as human beings
to mix with the object's ch'i and yün, we open ourselves to experiencing something beyond simple beauty. The word yün is also
used in the Tibetan language; their use of the term illustrates
how this can happen.

*"[The] essence of richness is called yün. Yün is actually a
traditional Tibetan term ... In eating good food, drinking
wine, or buying jewelry, there is a particular spot which hits
you. Or you find that if you see a gold coin, suddenly a particular aspect of it hits you as richness, which is its yün. It hits
you in the first thought—the basic thought."*

~ Chögyam Trungpa Rinpoche[11]

Trungpa Rinpoche also defined yün as "enriching presence."
The notion is that there are objects, places, and people whose
presences are so powerful that when we resonate with them,
we are enriched by the experience. The greater extent a work
of art possesses the felt presence of energy and harmony, ch'i
and yün, the greater its potential to cut through our personal
boundaries and create an experience that is shared by others.
This is something we can play with, as Chögyam Trungpa
encouraged his students to do. He called it a yün hunt, in

which we go shopping with other people and hunt for things that appear to have a strong enriching presence. It is not about finding the biggest, most expensive, shiny thing. Nor is it about possessing or purchasing it. Once you find it, you gather your companions to see if they can pick it out from its immediate environment. Most of us already do this when we bring along a friend to help us shop. If our goal is to outfit ourselves for a very important occasion or meeting, do we not instinctively shop for something with yün? Such shopping is based more on our felt sense than on information like brands and price. Due to our different styles and taste, of course, we will not always pick out the same thing. Crafts people, artisans, fine tailors, and anyone who makes the finest of things, bet their livelihood on whether or not we can feel yün.

The Philosophy of Sensuous Cognition

Our defining and clarifying presence, harmony, ch'i, and yün will help us to explore aesthetics and the transcendent experience: the sublime. Historically, the formal exploration of beauty and the aspects that constitute the specific characteristics in art that evoke a sense of beauty, has predominately fallen into the realm of aesthetics. In Kantian philosophy, aesthetics was a type of metaphysics concerned with the laws of perception. Aesthetics today can be defined as a philosophy of sensuous cognition, or the philosophy of beauty and its expression. Some see aesthetics as the study of psychological responses to beauty. Others, when overhearing a discussion on aesthetics, will simply walk out of the room for fear of being lost in the conversation or bored to death. Sadly, this response can be, in part, attributed to philosophers like Anthony Ashley Cooper, 3rd Earl of Shaftesbury, who took an analytical approach to art and criticism and who tried to morph aesthetics into a set of rules connecting beauty and morality. He also tried to instruct us on how we should think and feel, rather than providing tools to mine our own personal discoveries.

> *Art is not the application of a canon of beauty but what the instinct and the brain can conceive beyond any canon. When we love a woman we don't start measuring her limbs.*
>
> ~ Pablo Picasso[12]

In such aesthetic movements, there was no room for "out of the box" experiences. The aesthetic experience had to follow the cultural norm of those who expounded upon it. Insights would often be seen as erroneous views in need of rectification. Such restrictive approaches were obviously doomed from the beginning. I would argue that aesthetics can have a high purpose if it provides a path to appreciating our own direct, unfiltered, experience, as well as a means to communicate and share that experience with others.

When aesthetics becomes a thought sense trying to control a felt sense rather than something that illuminates a felt sense, it loses its authority. Aesthetics is best when it encourages us to allow sensuous cognition to precede our rationalizations. Then the reasoning that aesthetics offers can help us understand the experience. By understanding our experience of beauty, we create the ground for an even larger experience, which is the sublime experience.

The Sublime Experience

The sublime experience is described as one that is utterly complete, blissful, heavenly, and awe-inspiringly beautiful. In Sanskrit it would be called *sukha*, which is literally translated as "bliss."

The experience of beauty is primarily about felt sense; the sublime experience is about the experience of beauty *and* its appreciation. The sublime occurs when the experience of beauty arises within a field of knowledge and the two become one transcendental experience. From a meditation practitioner's view, this would occur when a nondual experience is sustained for more than a glimpse—when the observer and observed, subject and object, experiencer and experience, felt sense and thought sense are so united, it is as if they are one.

Although much of the experience of the sublime is beyond words, even in poetry, we can attempt to describe a meditative path towards it. It begins with synchronizing the mind and body in the present moment and coming back to original space in which we are awake, aware, and in tune with our environment. In this instance, our original space includes the work of art. As we experience the artwork, a thought sense is naturally generated. That thought sense is then informed by whatever knowledge we might possess. As it mixes with our felt sense, our felt sense is enriched and enlarged by it. That knowledge could be something about the work we recall, new information we have just read in an artist statement or program, something someone has shared with us, or it could be from any combination of sources.

Enriching information is married to our felt sense because it occurs *after* we have allowed ourselves to have our own direct experience. Therefore it informs and expands our appreciation. This is especially noticeable if we revisit the art and reexperience it within this enlarged and informed original space. The knowledge we possess is as much a part of the experience as anything. It is not something we are thinking about, it is merely what we know, just as we know what we feel. While revisiting the art, we can feel if what we have learned resonates with our experience or not. If it does, our felt sense grows and feeds a new thought sense.

Knowledge that comes into play after our direct experience does not narrow or filter our experience; rather, its very connection to the work serves to make our personal boundaries increasingly transparent—to the point of dissolving into the sublime experience. There is a true advantage to greater and greater knowledge, as long as it resonates with our direct experience. The more knowledge we include that resonates in this way with our initial and then expanded felt sense serves to fuel the next expansion. The sublime experience occurs when our felt and thought senses are serving each other as lovers making love. Imagine something like an ever-increasing and spinning *yin-yang* symbol in which one half is felt sense and the other half is thought sense. They fuel each other's expansion.

Figure 10: *Ever increasing and spinning yin-yang symbol*

An Experiment in the Sublime

As an example, we could engage in an experiment involving a specific work of art. It will be more of a thought experiment as you now read through because it will not yet involve the presence of the original painting or even an adequate reproduction, but it can serve as a model for engaging art and the sublime when you do go to a museum. If you are fortunate enough to be in Washington DC, you could visit the painting below at the National Gallery and try this exercise. As another intermediate measure, you can visit nga.gov and view images of the painting that are superior to those published here. Again, nothing really substitutes for being in the presence of a work of art, but for now, we have a representation.

As you gaze at the painting, you might recognize it, the artist, or recall its label. However, our goal is to engage the viewing process, as described in the previous chapter, and put everything we know aside for at least a brief moment to look at the painting as if for the first time with "fresh eyes." While we are doing this, our thoughts will likely barge their way back in, but we can let them go and come back to the painting in the same way as we come back to our breath after our thoughts steal us away during meditation practice. All we are doing is perceiving it literally, as it is.

We might find the space inside the painting is defined by the light, which places each object in the environment by illuminating it: the walls, the mirror, and the strands of pearls, the balance, a painting in the background as well as the woman and her expression. The relationships of light and dark, movement, temperature, the objects, and the woman all combine to share both a felt and thought sense of space, form, and energy in the form of a focus of interest: she is doing something with a balance.

It is not difficult to perceive the most immediate layer of the principles of space, form, and energy. As we continue to view the painting we might discover several other layers of these principles. All that we find works harmoniously to evoke a sense that we are looking at a moment of time. An untroubled moment, as her expression seems to convey. What does that feel like?

Figure 11: Woman Holding a Balance *by Johannes Vermeer*

We could just stop here and enjoy this much. Or we could go further. If we now introduce the title, the artist's name, and the time period it was painted, it would inform our experience, maybe a little or a great deal. It might cause us to spin off into judging its value historically and economically, the skill and technique of the artist, the limited palette of colors, etc. But we can bring ourselves gently back to the painting and reexperience it.

As long as we let such information come into play after we have had our experience of the work, then it will add to our experience rather than constrict it. After a few moments of revisiting the work, ideally with both fresh and informed eyes, we might gain an enlarged felt sense and a new appreciation for what might be going on within the painting. Our felt sense has danced a bit with our thought sense. We might note the small mirror on the wall that is facing her and that, like all mirrors, possesses both the felt and thought sense of reflectiveness (see Figure 12).

Figure 12: *Barely visible mirror on the wall under the window*

The woman herself appears to be reflecting on something as she holds a balance. The mirror and the balance reinforce one another as well as our experience of her as weighing something. Is she weighing material goods? Until recent microscopic examination, the painting was titled "The Goldweigher" or "Girl Weighing Pearls" because it was thought that the balance held jewels or coins. Today we know that the balance is empty, despite the presence of coins and jewelry on the table (see Figure 13). This knowledge and the resulting change in title must have changed the felt sense of the painting to those who knew it before and after. This changes our sense from one of weighing material goods to weighing or reflecting on something more deeply, psychologically. This could be an illustration of how knowledge can inform our felt sense of work of art.

Figure 13: *Detail of the woman holding a balance*

The arrangement of her clothing suggests that she might be pregnant. There is serenity in her expression. Her face is free from anxiety and fear. It is almost Madonna-like in its sense of understanding as she gazes at the balance (see Figure 14). Brain science shows that our feelings genuinely mirror the expressions of others, so we glimpse how she feels and we feel it also.

Figure 14: *Detail showing the woman's face*

Our thought sense again draws us further along to the question: *what is she weighing if not material goods?* The question invites further exploration. The background takes on greater importance in deepening our experience and appreciation. There is a barely visible painting behind her on the wall and just above her head, almost as if it were a caption of her thoughts. It is a painting of the Last Judgment in which God is located directly above her head (see Figure 15).

Figure 15: *Detail showing the Last Judgement*

This detail informs not only our thought sense of what is going on, but also our felt sense that she is weighing spiritual concerns in the face of the coins and the pearls, the material goods, laid out before her. Her untroubled expression with the balance in perfect equilibrium evokes a sense that she sees and feels material and spiritual things are in balance and by facing the mirror, that each reflects on the other. The imagery, which includes the lighting, the textures, the patina, the color, shapes and values, all generate felt senses followed by specific thought senses. These all combine to become an informed sensibility that is grander than the sum of their parts.

Each time we revisit this work, it builds on the previous experience and understanding. If we go with friends and share this exercise and hear their take on it, it will inform our view. Other eyes will take in different details and qualities. On other visitations we might take note of other aspects of the painting, such as the painter's use of white pigment to illuminate the scene and the style of melted edges, which make it appear as if the painting is illuminated from within. This produces a sense that it has a life of its own. Vermeer's use of the Golden Mean, an ancient Greek geometry based on the order found in nature, harmonizes the composition and makes it easier for us to harmonize with it.

The more we learn and return to share space with the work, the more encompassing our experience will be. It is no accident that upon viewing the very limited number of Vermeer's paintings in the world, individuals have swooned and waxed poetic about the great beauty they have seen and how sublime their experience was.

It is not difficult to see beauty, harmony, and a glimpse of the sublime in viewing such a Vermeer painting. It is, after all, a quiet figurative painting with recognizable images. But could we see and experience the same with a Picasso or a Pollock or the works of many of our contemporaries?

When Collings describes Matisse as achieving "sublime beauty" and Picasso's art as "savage," is he saying that we can experience the sublime with Matisse and not Picasso? I trust not. At the time in which he was painting, few described Matisse's works as sublime. Whereas today, few who appreciate modern art would say anything less. The difference between the two artists' work is that for many today, a Matisse is more accessible and attractive than a Picasso. Just as Picasso tested us to see ugly as beautiful, he still tests us to experience the sublime when things have become abstracted, if not estranged, from our conventions of everyday experience. Our learning and experience can serve to make us more rigid, reactionary, and narrow-minded, or it can open us up to all kinds of sublime experiences.

Seeking the sublime encourages us to realize that our felt and thought senses are of equal value. One is not better than the other; rather each defines and enriches the other. In Tibetan iconography the two principles are represented as being so entwined that they are represent in sexual union (see Figure 16).

Figure 16: *Samantabhadra and Samantabhadri in sexual union*

These two Buddhas represent a wisdom that is beyond form. Their nakedness represents the completely unadorned truth. *Samantabhadra* means "all pervasive goodness." As a male figure, he represents the wisdom of skillful means, knowledge, and the thought sense of everything. His female consort and equal,

Samantabhadri, represents wisdom itself, intuition, and the felt sense of everything. When these principles are joined in ourselves as lovers are joined, we are in bliss, sukka, and experiencing the sublime. However, because these Buddhas are enlightened, they are said to be in *maha sukka*. *Maha* means "great" in Sanskrit, and so *maha sukka* means "great bliss." This image shows us what is possible within our experience.

Figure 17: The Five Elements *by Sakyong Mipham Rinpoche*[1]

Chapter Thirteen

The Power of Display

Spontaneous, expressive art automatically has a universal
quality. That is why you do not have to go beyond anything.
If you see fully and directly, then that speaks, that
brings some understanding.

~ Chögyam Trungpa Rinpoche[2]

During the creative process, we move things about in space, shaping and reshaping them until what is important is seen and experienced. As part of the process, our results are naturally imbued with the space, form, and energy we give them. Making art is very much like a ritual in which we are making things sacred by assigning importance to them, by drawing attention to them. We empower the objects and performances we create to be art. What we call "art" is often displayed in special places in our homes, in galleries, museums, theaters, and performance halls, which can be seen as the shrines, temples, and churches of our art.

Art-Making is a Ritual

In many Native American, Aboriginal, and Tibetan ceremonies, objects are created, used, displayed and moved about during a ceremony. This is a dynamic real-time use of the principles of space, form, and energy. From a shamanistic view, each object, gesture, placement, and rearrangement of the *forms* during a ceremony serves to shape and reshape the *space* throughout the journey one is taking. Each change alters the *energy* of the environment, causing the participant's experience to evolve in specific ways: magical ways.

In this sense, magic does not mean tricks through which we deceive children and make fools of adults, but is understood as a means of working with our perceptions in real time to evoke a particular experience. The artist, or artist-as-shaman, starts with a state of mind and a vision, then creates objects or performances that communicate their vision, inspiration, discovery, or a sense of presence to the mind/heart of the viewer. This affects them, if not transforms them. What could be more magical than that?

Acknowledging Simplicity, Inviting Complexity

The principles of space, form, and energy by themselves are sufficient to display the simplicity and directness of our experience and our world, but they have their limits in that they offer a grand view with few specifics. If you can view one of the many Luminist or Hudson River School landscape painters of the late 1800s through early 1900s, such as the Albert Bierstadt painting, *Lake Lucerne*, 1858, you would see a scenic painting of a vast sky over an enormous western landscape, with a glowing sun. The painting as a whole is sharp, clear, and offers a powerful display, but many of the details are not within our grasp. It is an unmistakable example of the principles of space, form, and energy in a landscape painting. However, there are many different landscapes depicted in paintings, with various seasons and times of

The Power of Display

day. Different styles of applying the paint are used, and so on. The simplicity of the principles of space, form, and energy are elegant, comforting, and almost irresistible when confronted with the overwhelming complexity of our existence. But we only have to look around us to perceive the range of details, diversity, styles, and personalities that exist to see that the three principles do not help us to distinguish and define these aspects. Space, form, and energy are the bones of the creative and viewing processes, not the flesh.

A taste for simplicity cannot endure for long.

~ Eugène Delacroix[3]

Simplicity is a tool for us to leverage the unmanageable, but its purpose is not to deny the richness of our greater experience. Simplicity and complexity work together in transformative art.

I like a thing simple but it must be simple through complication. Everything must come into your scheme, otherwise you cannot achieve real simplicity.

~ Gertrude Stein[4]

The principles of space, form, and energy are, in essence, a linear relationship. If we see them in terms of heaven, earth and man principles—the heavens are above, earth is below, and humanity is between—in the creative and viewing processes, they naturally flow from one to another in linear fashion. Appreciating these three principles is part of seeing things as they are and how things manifest. Nevertheless, seeing things as they are is not just seeing the underlying simplicity, it is also perceiving any inherent complexity. As it turns out, what we

159

call "reality" is not only linear but also multidirectional, multi-cultural, and multidimensional.

To more fully see things as they are, we have to include the apparently limitless variety of all that we perceive. We cannot war with the existing complexity or retreat from it by saying, "It's too much!" If we do, we cut ourselves off from ever truly seeing the fullness and depth of things as they are in their numerous manifestations. Allowing the complexity into ourselves may feel like an enormous task, because it is, but there are things we can do to make it more manageable.

First, we may need to ask ourselves: what are we inviting complexity in to? Are we trying to cram more and more into an unchanging personal boundary that we established long ago? If we are to experience more than what we already know, a tight overstuffed mind is not the most receptive container. To expand our personal boundaries, if not transcend them, we need to favor inclusiveness over efficiency. A task that is easier said than done. It can feel quite scary to let go of our boundaries for even a brief moment and experience boundless openness.

I can still vividly recall a moment with my root[5] teacher while participating in a Buddhist Seminary. During a meeting with him, I found that we were staring into each other's eyes. I had a deep feeling that I was being invited to let go of a solid sense of self—the kind of letting go that takes place when we are in original space. As I relaxed and let go, I experienced this immense sense of physical and psychological expansion. After several moments, I felt that if I let go any further I would lose all reference point and any sense of my tiny notion of "me." So I became frightened and hesitated. With the next breath, I was being sucked back into myself.

160

What would it have been like to let it all go? Only having had a glimpse, I cannot say, but I know that, even after years of meditation practice, it was a challenge to let my everyday boundary expand to the point at which it might burst. As much diligence and bravery as this can take, I still feel it is more inviting to have an elastic and inclusive boundary than constantly maintaining a rigid self-centered one.

Art Within Interconnected Dynamic Systems

Once we decide to let the complexity in, the question becomes: how do we do it? Do we just let it all in, or is there some means, some contemplation or meditation-in-action to prevent us from feeling like we are being crushed or about to explode?

Let us first take a step back and look again at space, form, and energy. These three principles represent what could be called a "simple interconnected dynamic system." An interconnected dynamic system is an active system in which when one part is changed, all the other parts respond to one degree or another. You cannot change only one part without also changing the whole. You also cannot grasp the whole by separately scrutinizing the individual parts. The term *gestalt* is sometimes used to describe this. A gestalt is "a physical, biological, psychological, or symbolic configuration or pattern of elements so unified as a whole that its properties cannot be derived from a simple summation of its parts."[6] In other words, we cannot grasp anything unless we can perceive it in its native totality.

In many Eastern traditions, the term *mandala* is used. "A mandala is thus understood as the synthesis of numerous distinctive elements in a unified scheme, which through meditation can be recognized as the basic nature of existence."[7] Through meditation and the expansion of our view, we can learn to experience the details, diversity, and different styles of our experience as part of a whole, underlying reality. In Tibetan the term for mandala is *chi-chor*, which translates as "holding the essence or innermost nature."

The interconnected, dynamic system of our three principles of space, form, and energy is enormously helpful in making our creative and viewing processes more accessible; and yet too simple to accomplish the same for the complexity we experience. So we could invent a more inclusive and complex interconnected dynamic system customized for our own use, as the 1980s artist Jean-Michel Basquiat did, or immerse ourselves in a system that has existed for centuries—possibly even one based on a meditative or contemplative tradition. Cultures throughout history have developed and discovered complex interconnected dynamic systems that have expanded on the principles of space, form, and energy. For example, space is not just space. There are all types of space and spaciousness. We have experienced spaces that felt dead, others that felt alive, maybe electrified, others as spacious as a desert night sky or claustrophobic and seemingly solid as stone.

In addition to the unlimited appearances that forms take, they undergo changes from season to season, year to year, generation to generation. And there are styles through which energy manifests; it can be seductive, repulsive, comforting, inspiring, etc., as well as all the possible combinations of space, form, and energy when they are at play with one another.

Cultures have used such complex systems as a means to communicate not only all kinds of space, form, and energy, but their truths and the wealth of accumulated wisdoms in ways that transcend words. This communication manifests in various forms of display, such as dance, ritual, sculpture, mandala, monument, architecture, and so on. *Display* is defined as "holding something up for view in order to facilitate its communication and expression." As human beings, we display what we hold sacred—our culture, art, wisdom, and truths—not merely to reveal their surface characteristics, but to communicate a felt presence, life force, or ch'i. The languages of display are signs and symbols, because they communicate both information in terms of a thought sense and evoke an experience through a felt sense.

As a civilization, we are coming to realize what some of these ancient systems have represented for a long time—that our felt sense has a far greater influence on our thought sense than we ever imagined. This is pointed out in the documentary series called *Secret Life of the Brain*.[8] We are not merely thinking machines that occasionally feel, but feeling machines that also think. This undercuts the Cartesian model of mind and body, and the supremacy of rationalism. The psychological model of our thinking process as separate and distinct from our feeling process has recently been proven false by cognitive and neurological science. The notion that reason and logic should rule feelings and emotions turns out to be unreasonable and in truth, illogical. It has been shown that because of our biology, we cannot reason or make appropriate choices without our feelings being intimately involved. Our feeling sense informs our thinking process to such an extent that we cannot function properly without it.

Our memories of how we felt about previous choices, rather than what we thought, has a much greater influence on our current decision making than any logic or reason. We tend to make our decisions in this way and then struggle to find supporting logic. In science, it is not yet clear how feelings and emotions generate thoughts, or how thoughts generate emotions, but we do know they are inextricably linked and that each is a part of one whole.

It is because this is true that a display can be so powerful. It seems the more skillfully they are created, the more we are drawn to and affected by them. Displays attempt to reach the whole of our being: felt sense and thought sense simultaneously. It can be as simple as the Chinese pictograph for "emperor," which consists of three horizontal lines that stand for heaven, earth, and man, and one vertical line that connects the three indicating that it is the emperor that joins heaven, earth, and man.

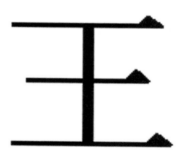

Figure 18: *The Chinese character for "emperor"*

Or a display can be as fantastic, complex, and rich as the ceiling of the Sistine Chapel or a Kalachakra Mandala.

Figure 19: *Tibetan Buddhist Kalachakra sand mandala*

Inclusive Versus Exclusive Systems

There are two types of complex interconnected dynamic systems: inclusive and exclusive systems. Their differences lie in how they were created. Exclusive systems are often conceptual fabrications, or belief systems, superimposed on reality in order to rationalize it. The parts that work within the predetermined format are included, and what does not work is ignored. An exclusive system is rigid and its strengths are determined more by what is excluded than what is included. Its self-limiting and inflexible nature would make it incompatible with a desire to expand our boundaries.

An inclusive system is one that is infinitely expandable and its value is based more on what it includes than excludes. Inclusive systems that are based on the accumulation of direct experience, and the wisdom that flows from experience, can assist us in expanding our boundaries.

The mandala in Figure 19 is part of a long meditative tradition, and it describes the nature of the cosmos and a wide array of possible experiences, states of mind, styles, and wisdoms. Its elaborateness is an attempt to encompass as much of the fullness of things as they are as possible. One central aspect of this interconnected dynamic system is that it includes four different gates or entrances: east, west, north, and south. They can be seen within the square structure and they are colored respectively as white, red, orange, and black. Each entrance embodies the welcoming of a divergent view, style, and energy from the "four corners" of the earth. The three dimensional version of the mandala includes all directions of the universe.

This is an example of its inclusive nature because all types of experiences are invited into it as opposed to being prescreened and filtered. In principle, a mandala is infinitely expandable because it is a state of mind as much as it is anything. Therefore, it can become a tool for unlimited growth and understanding as one studies the mandala and practices the meditations associated with it.

Systems That Reflect Innate Qualities

When you choose a system to explore, it is also important to determine if the system is based primarily on concept. If it is not grounded in experience, it will have little power, magic, or transformative value for us. For the most part, our civilization has disowned and distanced itself from systems of the past such as mandalas. Surviving cultures that attempt to convey felt sense as much as thought sense are often considered primitive, naive, unscientific, and filled with superstitions. And yet, every aspect of our culture is permeated with their observations, truths, and accompanied felt sense. Color can serve as an example of a connection to past systems and their wisdoms, specifically red and blue.

Today, color can be scientifically measured for its wavelength and temperature. Red is near infrared on the spectrum, which is physically warmer than the other colors. Infrared lamps are commonly used today to keep food warm. Compared to blue, red is significantly hotter. Optically, when both colors are side by side on a neutral ground, red appears to be closer to us than blue. This is said to be because of the location of the red cone receptors in the eye. Red literally appears to be coming toward us when compared to cooler colors like blue, which appear to recede and feel more spacious.

In a less scientific time, when such effects on physiology were unmeasured, red was associated, and still is today, with fire, blood, and passion, all of which radiate warmth or heat. Surveys have shown that red is the most popular color, and we are drawn to it much as a moth to a flame. How can a Greek or Eurocentric philosophy based on logic alone account for the fact that a plant placed near the color red grows measurably toward it or that the color red makes our hearts beat faster and the color blue lowers our blood pressure? It is no accident that many fire engines are painted red or that stop signs and automobile taillights are red. People used to claim red was the logical color choice for fire engines because it stands out, however, red at night, unless illuminated, appears dark gray. Yellow is a more logical color choice for day and nighttime visibility, yet many still use red on emergency vehicles. It is because our felt sense of red is more strongly associated with fire and emergencies than yellow.

It is no surprise that blue is connected with the heavens in most religions. Many deities around the world are pictured either wearing blue or are themselves blue in color to evoke a felt sense of the heavens. Phrases in our language indicate heavenly associations with the color blue: cordon bleu, blue ribbon, or blue blood indicating excellence, nobility, or being "heavenly appointed." The more we study color and its associations, we find that we are powerfully affected and influenced by it; something that interconnected dynamic systems of the past like the Kalachakra Mandala have displayed for centuries.

If we wish to have a guide to assist us with our exploration, it is important to pick a system that we resonate with and that is connected to actual experience in order to facilitate a deeper and more expansive connection to our world. The Four Elements, the Five Elements, a gestalt, a mandala, the Four Directions, the Four Seasons, the Five Buddha Families, the Six Realms of Existence, the Four Dignities of Shambhala, astrology, feng shui, and other displays found around the world are examples of complete, traditional, interconnected dynamic systems that are available to us to explore. The intent behind these systems of display has been for the betterment of a culture and its people—and in some instances to understand our relationship to the cosmos.

Yet they can also be misused. This generally happens when some of the more elaborate traditional systems are entirely self-taught, without the benefit of feedback from an accomplished master. An authentic, skillful, and compassionate teacher not only conveys information, offers balance, and fosters insights that might otherwise be blocked by our fixations, but also acts to keep us from harm.

Attempting to learn the vast wealth of accumulated wisdom contained within a particular system can be both inspiring and daunting. An apprentice can readily become overwhelmed and fall back on memorization and efficiency by trying to pick out the salient points, all the while losing the whole for a sum of the edited parts. Misuse can also result when our desire for simplicity seduces us into mapping the apparent characteristics of multiple systems into one simpler, overarching system. Each system arose and evolved within a particular culture and there will be aspects that are unique to that system. Differing cultural signage often cannot be successfully mapped in an effort to get to a common symbolism. You cannot get to one culture's symbolism through another's signs. Each culture's system is autonomous and designed to be understood as a whole in and of itself, and most importantly, from *within* itself. A rudimentary appreciation can occur from external study of a system as if one were an archeologist studying artifacts. However, if our desire is to experience a system so that we can make use of it in our creative and viewing processes, it is best accomplished from within its own parameters.

When we immerse ourselves in a traditional system, it reveals not only complex signs and symbols, but also illuminates our personality, style, unique nature, and what we could call our "basic nature." In our effort to see things as they fully are, we cannot exclude ourselves from this path of exploration and we must reflect on our own character as an individual explorer. Our path reflects how we uniquely experience our world, as well as how we distinctly express ourselves.

Science attributes our individual differences to learning, culture, and genetics. All clearly have a major role to play. We are not stagnant entities and our interaction with the world changes us as much as anything. Neuroscience has found that conscious awareness and experience literally change the genetic nature, the DNA, of the biology of the brain. These altered genes are not genes of the reproductive system that can be passed on, but they are altered genes that end up determining significant differences between even the most similar among us. Therefore a truly shared, completely objective response between people is biologically impossible as well as logically impossible.

All this furthers the notion that the most we can share is our objective subjectivity, in which we are as objective as possible about our subjectivity. This provides the possibility of seeing through our subjectivity to some commonality of vision. In this way, our differences are something to be realized and enjoyed; after all it is our differences that entice us to discover, create, communicate, and share.

The Purpose Is Illumination

An interconnected dynamic system can illuminate our world, but also the specifics of our personality, subjectivity, and individuality. They provide a means to glimpsing the viewpoints and the truths of others in order to achieve a richer and more complete view. This is why we can learn to truly enjoy art forms that are different from our own, even entirely outside our comfort zone. Acknowledging our subjectivity allows us to see our part of the picture as *part* of a picture. If we are motivated to discover the balance of the picture, then we will have to reach out and absorb other viewpoints and allow them to inform ours. What makes an interconnected system *dynamic* and of value to us is that it encourages us to be inclusive, inquisitive, and experimental by viewing multiple points of view as accumulated wealth rather than criticisms or challenges.

The exploration of an interconnected dynamic system can reveal our deep loyalty to our specific view and how offensively or defensively we act to protect it. As it turns out, we cannot begin to relax our boundaries so they may expand to include more unless we know what and where those boundaries are. It is a process of self-discovery in which we are trying to find out who we truly are, as opposed to who we think we are or wish we could be. Who we are determines what we create and what we display. If we are trying to consciously or unconsciously be something other than who we are, our creative process and its results reflect precisely that. We are on display as much as the artwork we create. We can be an artful display or one full of artifice. Discovering who we are provides the possibility of making this choice in our display.

When it comes to how we manifest ourselves, there are three aspects that contribute to who we are. The first is what could be seen as our basic nature. It is a "home base" that includes how we perceive and experience our world—our objective subjectivity. Next is our expressive nature: how we express ourselves. This might have a completely different style from our basic nature. Finally, there is our neurotic nature. Our neurotic nature is what manifests when we do not like or trust who we are and we superimpose the behavior of people we admire onto ourselves. No matter how adept we are at pretending, we are not being authentic, and at some point the people who know us well will see through it. We might even come to realize we are not fooling anyone, but we feel driven to continue in the vain hope that our mask is still somehow better than our original face.

The goal of seeing ourselves as we are by illuminating our basic, expressive, and neurotic natures is to make us acutely aware of the differences between who we are and any artifice. The awareness of artifice alone, which is the direct result of a meditation discipline, is a transformative tool. When we arrive at moments when we are who we are without pretense—which occurs within original space—we naturally express with energy and power and what we create reflects that. The energy that was tied up and wasted in pretense is now available for creativity.

Let's take a look at one complex interconnected dynamic system, the Four Seasons. In your mind's eye, experience each season as they occur in North America, most of Europe, and areas of the world with similar latitudes. Examine each season in detail, in terms of its felt and thought sense. You may discover that the seasons appear to have four types of personalities and that one particular season relates to your personality more than the others.

For example, call to mind an Ansel Adams winter scene: cold, crisp with sharp edges, black, white, and gray. Now contrast that with a seductive, colorfully saturated, springtime garden in which everything is flowering and flowing into each other—as found in later paintings by Claude Monet. Some of us might identify with the warmth and flowing, seductive quality of the Monet and find the winter scene forbidding, cold, and aloof. Others might find the painted garden scene a bordello of nature—garish, unrealistic, and overbearing—while the winter scene strikes them as crisp, pure, clean, and refreshing in its simplicity. What we genuinely identify with does not make us or it right or wrong. It merely helps to identify and appreciate our basic nature and style.

If we study and practice astrology, we see our sun sign as a description of our basic nature and our rising sign as how we express it. If we are interested in the mandala of the Five Buddha Families of the Buddhist Mahamudra tradition, we find ourselves identifying with one of the Buddha families for our basic nature, another for how we express ourselves, and yet another for our style of neurosis. The same would be true for the Five Elements: earth, water, fire, wind, and space. It makes no difference whether any of these interconnected dynamic systems have a physical reality in themselves, beyond what we give them. No one has located the mind as a physical organ, but that has not stopped us from exploring and using it.

We all must have had conversations in which we found ourselves frustrated—if not angry, feeling unheard and, as a result, shouting our point of view, thinking that saying our truth louder and repeatedly will somehow get the other person to finally hear us and agree with us. More often than we would like to admit, they did hear us and *do* understand what we are saying, but simply disagree. By developing mindfulness and awareness in meditation and extending that into meditation-in-action, we begin to recognize our subjectivity, our style, our biases. Most importantly, we also come to see through them, which provides the opportunity to move beyond them and therefore make the most challenging situations workable.

Interconnected dynamic systems encourage us to see our experience and our world, with all its richness and diversity, from as many points of view as possible. The greater the diversity of art forms we can learn to experience through both our felt and thought senses, the nearer we come to experiencing what "art"—or anything in life—truly is. Achieving a greater perspective not only helps us discover whole worlds of new experiences and appreciations, but as creative people we gain an ever-expanding palette for creative expression.

The Originality of Our Particular Wisdom

The expansion of our boundaries and the inclusion of complexity best occur in the space of meditation and meditation-in-action practice. In the meditative traditions I have experienced, no matter how elaborate the practice, it was surrounded by and permeated with a simple and direct meditation practice like the one described in this book. Without such a simple practice, the complexity we experience can become confusion instead of insight and wisdom. It is with the foundation of a meditative practice, which comes as close as we can to doing nothing while being awake and aware, that we come to see things as they are and know ourselves as we are. The spaciousness we experience within such a practice allows us to see through our thoughts and storylines to the substance of the things themselves. It is within this space that originality springs forth, without effort. It simply arises and, if so inspired, takes shape in our imagination. Then, if we choose to, we give it form until it has its own energy and life as art. When we view the result, we celebrate what it communicates.

When we embrace who we truly are, we have a path to express ourselves with pure expression, spontaneously and without self-consciousness. As our boundaries stretch, they become thinner and more transparent so that there is less between us and our experience. We become more intimate with our world, as would new lovers and old friends, until there is no separation between the experience and the experiencer. It is from this place that the art we make can speak powerfully and with dignity.

Notes

Chapter One: A Place to Land

1. Constantin Brancusi and Carola Giedion-Welcker, *Constantin Brancusi* (Basel: B. Schwabe, 1958) 240.

Chapter Two: The Importance of Doing Nothing

1. Rita Carter, *Exploring Consciousness* (Berkeley: University of California Press 2002) 320.

2. Chögyam Trungpa Rinpoche and Judy L. Leif, *The Art of Calligraphy: Joining Heaven & Earth* 1st ed. (Boston: Shambhala, 1994) viii, 173.

3. Russell T. Hurlburt, "Telling What We Know: Describing Inner Experience, Trends in Cognitive Sciences," 5:9 (September 2001) 400-403.

4. A Koan is a Zen Buddhist riddle contemplated during meditation to develop intuitive knowledge.

Chapter Four: Perception is More Important than Talent

1. From the foreword in this book, xvii.

2. Rita Carter, *Exploring Consciousness* (Berkeley: University of California Press, 2002) 320.

3. Stephen L. Macknik and Susana Martinez-Conde, with Sandra Blakeslee. "Mind over Magic?" *Scientific American Mind*, Nov/Dec 2010.

4. W. Wayt Gibbs, "Side Splitting: Jokes, Ice Water and Magnetism Can Change Your View of the World—Literally". Scientific American Magazine. 2001.

5. Widely attributed to Taisen Deshimaru.

Chapter Five: Felt Sense and Thought Sense

1. Vincent Lobrutto, *Stanley Kubrick: A Biography* (De Capo Press, 1999) 284.
2. Paul Klee and Felix Klee, *The Diaries of Paul Klee, 1898-1918* (Berkeley: University of California Press, 1964) xx, 424.
3. Timothy Wilson, *Strangers to Ourselves: Discovering the Adaptive Unconscious* (Harvard University Press, 2002).
4. Guy Claxton, *Hare Brain, Tortoise Mind: Why Intelligence Increases When You Think Less.* 1st Ecco ed. (Hopewell, NJ: Ecco Press, 1999) xi, 259.
5. Chögyam Trungpa Rinpoche, *Glimpses of Abhidharma.* First ed. (Vajradhatu, Boulder CO, 1975) 100.
6. Malcolm Gladwell, *Blink: The Power of Thinking Without Thinking.* 1st ed. (New York: Little, Brown and Co., 2005) viii, 277.
7. Robert Andrews, *The New Penguin Dictionary of Modern Quotations.* 2 ed. (New York: Penguin Books, 2001) 588.

Chapter Six: Self-Expression and Pure Expression

1. Shunryu Suzuki-Roshi, a Japanese Zen priest belonging to the Soto lineage. He came to San Francisco in 1959 at the age of fifty-four and settled there. Zen Center came into being and he was its first abbot. Under his tutelage, Zen Center grew into City Center, Green Gulch Farm, and Tassajara Zen Mountain Center. He was undoubtedly one of the most influential Zen teachers of his time. Some of his edited talks have been collected in the books *Zen Mind, Beginner's Mind* and *Branching Streams Flow in the Darkness: Zen Talks on the Sandokai.* Suzuki-Roshi died in 1971.

2. Duncan Williams, *The Trousered Ape*. 1971. (New Rochelle, NY: Arlington House Publishers, 1971)

3. There are eight types of consciousness described in most philosophical schools based on the *Abhidharma*. The most influential school has been *Yogachara* (mind only). In this school, the first six consciousnesses are the six sense perceptions previously discussed. The seventh consciousness is our self-referencing and the experience of an "I." The eighth consciousness is referred to as the storehouse or the ground basis of consciousness itself and is similar to what is referred to in Western psychology as the "unconscious." Although all eight play their part in creating a total sense of an "I" or ego, it is the seventh that creates the sense of continuity and pride in itself: egotism.

    The eighth consciousness also accounts for our personalities and style, which affects how each of us takes in information and experiences differently from one another. It also defines our individual differences in how we express ourselves. It explains why two or more people, even when attempting to be objective, will still tend to describe the same thing differently.

4. Sakyong Mipham Rinpoche, *1999 Seminary Transcripts: Teachings from the Sutra Tradition, Book Two*. (Halifax: Vajradhatu Publications)

5. Rita Carter, *Exploring Consciousness* (Berkeley: University of California Press, 2002) 320.

Chapter Seven: Originality, Creativity, and Spontaneity

1. Caroline Blinder, *A Self-made Surrealist: Ideology and Aesthetics in the Work of Henry Miller* (Boydell & Brewer Press, 2000) 170.

2. Franz Kafka and Malcolm Pasley, *Shorter works [of] Franz Kafka*. (London: Secker & Warburg, 1973).

3. John Lennon, "Beautiful Boy (Darling Boy)," released on the 1980 album *Double Fantasy*. Cited in *The Columbia World of Quotations*

(Davis Library Electronic Reference).

4. Gilbert, as quoted in *Independent* (London: April 17, 1989).

5. Henri Matisse, *The Columbia Dictionary of Quotations* (Columbia University Press, 1954, 1993, 1995).

6. Alan Watts, *Zen and the Art of the Controlled Accident*. Recorded on Mystic Fire Audio, 1970.

Chapter Eight: Signs and Symbols

1. Paul Klee and Felix Klee, *The Diaries of Paul Klee, 1898-1918* (Berkeley: University of California Press, 1964) xx, 424.

2. In Zen Buddhism, Zazen means "seated meditation." Zazen is very similar to, but more formal than, the meditation described in this book.

3. As quoted in *Real Magic: Creating Miracles in Everyday Life* by Wayne W. Dyer (New York, NY: HarperTorch, 1993) 123.

4. Steve Kroft interview with Henri Cartier-Bresson. *60 Minutes: Cartier-Bresson* (CBS: Season 28, Episode 35, May 12, 1996).

5. Tor Nørretranders, *The User Illusion* (New York: Penguin, 1999).

6. "Symbol," *Encyclopaedia Britannica*, 15th edition. 1994-2002.

7. Alfred Korzybski, *Science and Sanity; An Introduction to Non-Aristotelian Systems and General Semantics*, 4th ed. , Lakeville, CT: International Non-Aristotelian Library Pub. Co.; distributed by Institute of General Semantics, 1958, 806.

8. Chögyam Trungpa Rinpoche, *Cutting Through Spiritual Materialism* (Boston: Shambhala Publications, 2002) 256.

9. In a way, the two truths of relative truth and absolute truth are one of the foundations of the second most important Buddhist philosophical school, *Madhyamika*, the middle way, with *Yogachara* being its rival. Madhyamika was a school of Buddhist philosophy founded

by Nararjuna around the third century. It reached great importance in India, Tibet, China, and Japan and is the basis for many schools of Buddhist philosophy and psychology today. It was especially concerned with the "two truths," relative and absolute truth and their relationship. Their relationship is similar to the relationship between knowledge and direct experience, as well as sign and symbol.

Yogachara literally means "application of yoga" and became known as the "mind only" school of Buddhism because of its focus on the nature of perceptions, consciousness, and the experience of reality. It was founded by Asanga around the fourth century. Its philosophy became the center of the great sixth century university in Northern India, Nalanda. Yogacharan philosophy not only has its own schools today and is reflected in this book, but the results of some cognitive science experiments appear to support their views regarding perception and consciousness.

10. Chögyam Trungpa Rinpoche and Judy L. Lief, *Dharma Art*. 1st ed. (Boston: Shambhala Publications, 1996) xiv, 144.

11. Joseph Kosuth, *One and Three Chairs (Une et Trois Chaises)*. 1965.

12. Duchamp's "readymade" sculptures were everyday objects, but were placed into various settings, such as a gallery, so they would be looked at as aesthetic objects.

13. Chögyam Trungpa Rinpoche and Judy L. Lief, *Dharma Art*. 1st ed. (Boston: Shambhala Publications, 1996) xiv, 144.

14. Gary Gach, ed. *What Book!?: Buddha Poems from Beat to Hiphop* (Berkeley: Parallax Press, 1998).

Chapter Nine: The Creative Process as Meditation-in-Action

1. Reginald H. Blyth, Haiku. Vol. 1. (Tokyo: Kamakura Bunko, 1949).

2. *Élan vital*, was coined by French philosopher Henri Bergson in his 1907 book *Creative Evolution*. It was translated in the English edition as *vital impetus*, or "life force." Bergson linked it closely with

consciousness. Today some see it as similar to ch'i.

3. *Ch'i* literally means "air," "vapor," "breath," "ether," or "energy" and it refers to the vital energy or life force that pervades and enlivens all things. Hsieh-Ho, a painter and critic during the sixth century who lived in Nanking, wrote the *Six Canons of Art*. Five of them had to do with discipline and technique. The first canon on which all the others depended had to do with what cannot be learned but only discovered through an intuitive process. The first canon reads *ch'i yun sheng tung,* with a literal translation of "spirit rhythm life movement."

4. *Prana* is Sanskrit for "breath" or "the breath of life."

5. Diana Kan and Miriam Mermey, *The How and Why of Chinese Painting* (New York, NY: Van Nostrand Reinhold Co., 1974) 175.

6. Brewster Ghiselin, *The Creative Process, A Symposium* (Berkeley: University of California Press, 1952) 259.

7. Wade Graham, "At Play with Night and Day in the Desert," *Los Angeles Times Magazine*, February 17, 2002.

Chapter Ten: The Viewing Process

1. Robert L. Solso, *Cognition and the Visual Arts* (Cambridge, MA: MIT Press, 1994) xvi, 294.

2. Richard Whittaker, "Greeting the Light, an Interview with James Turrell." *Works + Conversations, A Journal of the Society for the ReCognition of Art,* Vol. 2.

3. *Where Poems Come From.* Video, Lannan Foundation , 1991.

4. Eugene T. Gendlin, *Focusing.* 1st ed. (New York, NY: Everest House, 1978) vi, 178.

5. Leo Tolstoy, *What is Art?* (London: Penguin Books, 1995) 201.

Chapter Eleven: Conditional and Unconditional Beauty

1. "Beauty," *Merriam-Webster Unabridged Dictionary*. Online edition, accessed 2002.

2. "Art," *The American Heritage Dictionary of the English Language*. 4th ed., 2000.

3. Ingrid Fisher-Schreiber, F.-K.E., Kurt Friedrichs, & Michael S. Diener, *The Encyclopedia of Eastern Philosophy and Religion*. First ed, ed. G.W. Stephan Schuhmacker. (Boston: Shambhala Publications, 1994) 468.

4. Shinsuke Shimojo and Ladan Shams, "Sensory Modalities are Not Separate Modalities: Plasticity and Interactions." *Current Opinion In Neurobiology* (2001; Vol. 11 [114]) 505-509.

5. Ivar A. Richards, *Practical Criticism, A Study of Literary Judgment.* (New York, NY: Harcourt, Brace, 1950) xiii, 375.

6. George Orwell and Herman Finkelstein Collection, *Nineteen Eighty-Four, A Novel.* 1st American ed. (New York, NY: Harcourt, 1949) 314.

7. "Beauty," *Merriam-Webster Unabridged Dictionary*. Online edition, accessed 2002.

8. Chögyam Trungpa Rinpoche and J. L. Leif, *The Art of Calligraphy: Joining Heaven & Earth.* 1st ed. (Boston: Shambhala Publications, 1994) viii, 173.

9. Emily Dickinson and T. H. Johnson, *The Complete Poems of Emily Dickinson.* (Boston: Back Bay Books, Little, Brown and Co., 1997) xiii, 770.

10. Mathew Collings, *This is Modern Art.* (New York, NY: Watson-Guptill Publications, 2000).

Chapter Twelve: Presence and the Sublime

1. Dave Hickey, *The Invisible Dragon/Four Essays on Beauty.* 1st ed. (Los Angeles: Art Issues Press, 1993) 64.

2. W. Somerset Maugham, *Cakes and Ale.* 1st Vintage International ed. (New York, NY: Vintage International, 2000) 308.

3. Albert Camus, P. M. W. Thody, and J. O'Brien, *Notebooks.* 1st Marlowe & Co. ed. (New York: Marlowe & Co., 1995).

4. Chögyam Trungpa Rinpoche and Judy L. Leif, *The Art of Calligraphy: Joining Heaven & Earth.* 1st ed. (Boston: Shambhala Publications, 1994) viii, 173.

5. Dave Hickey, *The Invisible Dragon/Four Essays on Beauty.* 1st ed. (Los Angeles: Art Issues Press, 1993) 64.

6. Hsieh Ho, *Six Canons of Painting.* c 500-c. 535 C.E.

7. Fritz V. Briessen, *The Way of the Brush; Painting Techniques of China and Japan.* (Tokyo, Rutland, VT: C.E. Tuttle Co., 1962) 329.

8. Ingrid Fisher-Schreiber, F.-K.E., Kurt Friedrichs, and Michael S. Diener, *The Encyclopedia of Eastern Philosophy and Religion.* First ed, ed. by G.W. Stephan Schuhmacker. (Boston: Shambhala Publications, 1994) 468.

9. Jackson Pollack, *From Possibilities 1.* Winter of 1947-48, Wittenborn, Schultz, Inc.

10. Wucious Wong, *The Tao of Chinese Landscape Painting: Principles & Methods.* 1st ed. (New York: Design Press, 1991) 176.

11. Chögyam Trungpa Rinpoche, "Golden Key II: Rousing a Mind of Delight and Richness," *Kalapa Assembly Talks,* October 15, 1978.

12. Museum of Modern Art and Alfred H. Barr, *Picasso, Fifty Years of His Art.* (New York, NY: The Museum of Modern Art, 1946) 314.

Chapter Thirteen: The Power of Display

1. The circle represents the element of water, the square represents the element of earth, the semi-circle represents the element of fire, the triangle represents the element of air or wind, and the images in the center represent the element space. The images in the center are: On top is the stroke of Ashe, which represents confidence and dignity and the image below it is the Sanskrit seed syllable "Ah," which is said to be the first sound we utter and the last when we die.

2. Chögyam Trungpa Rinpoche, *Cutting Through Spiritual Materialism* (Boston: Shambhala Publications, 2002) 256.

3. Eugene Delacroix and Walter Pach, *The Journal of Eugene Delacroix* (New York, NY: Covici, Friede, 1937) 731.

4. Robert Haas, *What are Masterpieces?* (New York: Pitman Publishing Corporation, 1979).

5. One's root teacher is also known as one's "guru" in Vajrayana Buddhism, as in many other teachings. Your root teacher is said to be the one who properly introduces you to your world, and it is from this view that all subsequent teachings, and teachers, are understood.

6. "Gestalt," *The American Heritage Dictionary of the English Language,* 4th ed., 2000.

7. Ingrid Fisher-Schreiber, F.-K.E., Kurt Friedrichs, and Michael S. Diener, *The Encyclopedia of Eastern Philosophy and Religion.* 1st ed, ed. by G.W. Stephan Schuhmacker. (Boston: Shambhala Publications, 1994) 468.

8. WNET (Television station : New York N.Y.) and David Grubin Productions., *The Secret Life of the Brain.* 2001, New York, NY:

Thirteen/WNET.

Acknowledgments

Publishing a second book has reinforced my experience that this process is a collaborative one. And why should it be otherwise when there are so many wonderful and talented people to make a contribution. Some of those who have encouraged me to write this book, and who made its publication possible are: my wife, Anne, who takes nothing for granted and keeps me on my toes; my son, who helped me see what I wrote through another generation's eyes; my first teacher, the late Vietnamese Zen Buddhist Master, Dr. Thien-An; my root guru and founder of Shambhala Buddhism, the late Vidyadhara, Chögyam Trungpa Rinpoche, who is the source and inspiration for so much of this book; and his son, my current teacher Sakyong Mipham Rinpoche, who helps me understand, appreciate, and practice the teachings of my root guru.

Teachers and students in Shambhala Art have helped me understand how it is possible to convey not only the thought sense of a teaching, but its felt sense. Stanley Weiser taught me how to be a better writer without knowing it, or maybe he did. April Smith generously read multiple drafts and helped me find a way to cut this book to a manageable size. The friendship of David Luce, my colleague, has helped me wrap my mind around so many contemporary art issues.

The thoughtful contributions of my editor, Jennifer Holder, made an immeasurable difference as the book journeyed from draft to publication. Much gratitude to her for assembling a great production team and coordinating the process: I would like to thank my book designer, Gail Nelson; meticulous proof-reader, Darla Upchurch; patient cover designer, Beth Skelley; and printer liaison, Jerry Gentry.

About the Author

Steven Saitzyk is an adjunct professor of humanities and sciences at one of the leading art colleges in North America, Art Center College of Design in Pasadena. He is also an artist, former biochemist, and author of *Art Hardware*, a book about the nature of materials for art-making. He is a former columnist for the artists' magazines *Site Local* and *Visions*. He has studied and worked directly with some of the leading contemporary artists of our time, as well as masters of Buddhist art, meditation, philosophy, and psychology, among them the Venerable Vidyadhara, Chögyam Trungpa Rinpoche, and Sakyong Mipham Rinpoche. He has attended a Buddhist Seminary and has practiced meditation for more than thirty-five years, as well as consulted and lectured on meditation, Dharma Art, Shambhala Art, Vajrayana Buddhism and its iconography, Tibetan art, symbolism, and the materials used to create both Asian art and art of the Western world. He is one of the founders of Shambhala Art, a nonprofit arts education program designed to integrate meditation and contemplation with the creative and viewing processes. He is its current international director. Visit ShambhalaArt.org. You may see his artwork at StevenSaitzyk.com.